The Society of
St Vincent de Paul in Ireland

The Society of

ST VINCENT DE PAUL

in IRELAND

170 Years of Fighting Poverty

edited by
Bill Lawlor & Joe Dalton

The Society of Saint Vincent de Paul

170

Years of Charity & Justice
Since 1844

NEW ISLAND

The Society of St Vincent de Paul in Ireland:
170 Years of Fighting Poverty

First published in 2014
by New Island Books
16 Priory Hall Office Park
Stillorgan
County Dublin
Republic of Ireland

www.newisland.ie

PRINT ISBN: 978-1-84840-256-0
EPUB ISBN: 978-1-84840-257-7
MOBI ISBN: 978-1-84840-258-4

British Library Cataloguing Data. A CIP catalogue record for this book is available from the British Library.

Typeset by JVR Creative India
Cover design by New Island Books
Printed by ScandBook AB, Sweden

Contents

Preface

by Geoff Meagher

'I am asking the volunteers of the Society of St Vincent de Paul to look after people who have too many needs and not enough rights, people who demand with reason a fuller share in public affairs, security in work and safeguards against poverty.'

Those were the words of Blessed Frédéric Ozanam in 1833 when he founded the Society of St Vincent de Paul in Paris. The society was established in Ireland eleven years later, and faced a major challenge shortly afterwards when the Great Famine of 1845 occurred.

In the 170 years since its foundation, the SVP in Ireland has continued to help those in need, including through two world wars, the War of Independence, the Civil War and periods of intense economic and social strife.

The work of the Society depends upon the thousands of volunteer members in every parish in Ireland who, without fail, carry it out every day, every week, of every year.

This book records the Society's work through the experiences of its members and, as such, is a unique record. Our members are supported by dedicated professional staff, necessary in modern times as they respond to the needs of the deprived in a nation where the words of

Frédéric Ozanam in 1842 are as relevant today as they were then.

The SVP is dedicated to the concept of social justice: equality of opportunity for everyone. Social justice must be at the centre of a nation that cares for all of its people equally.

We will continue to work towards achieving this difficult goal.

I thank those involved in the production of this first book about the work of the volunteers of the Society of St Vincent de Paul in Ireland, published in the 170th year of its existence in this country. To all those volunteers who contributed to it, to Bill Lawlor and Joe Dalton who compiled it, Tom MacSweeney who initiated the publication, to Eoin Purcell, the Commissioning Editor of New Island, who saw it through to production, his staff and editors, to all involved, the thanks of the Society. To all those who read it, I hope it provides an understanding of the work of the SVP in Ireland and, perhaps, stimulates you to consider joining or assisting the Society's work.

Geoff Meagher
National President,
Society of St Vincent de Paul in Ireland, 2014

Foreword

Fiona Looney

I grew up in Greenhills, South Dublin, in a parish that – as our priests liked to remind us – boasted one of the largest annual collections for the Society of St Vincent de Paul in the country. They would mention this every year, at the start of December, just before the wicker collection baskets with the distressed green-cushioned lining were passed around. It became, I suppose, a sort of annual challenge: if we had rattled the record books the previous year, then we would positively set them alight this Christmas. And we did. Every year, for as long as I lived in that parish, we bettered ourselves.

And it wasn't as if we had much money. Years later, I heard, anecdotally, that the only parish in the Dublin diocese to come close to matching our contribution was Dun Laoghaire, an area which had many pockets of affluence, all of them apparently deep.

But Greenhills was very different. By the time I reached secondary school at the start of the 1980s, the oil crisis of the 1970s had efficiently converted itself into a savage economic recession that blighted working class areas like ours. It was almost unheard of for girls in my school to have two parents working, and as we navigated our way unsteadily through that period of high unemployment, the number of my peers who had a parent working at all steadily dropped.

And all the time, we kept giving more money to the St Vincent de Paul. Sometimes, when I tell people now about that time and that place, they find it odd that people who effectively had no spare cash were such enthusiastic supporters of any charity. To outsiders, it must have been the equivalent of famine victims in Africa setting up a direct debit to Concern.

But the SVP never felt like charity to us. The other organisation that thrived in our parish during those bleak years was the local credit union, and in many respects the approach to both institutions was the same. Times were hard and money was short, so everyone threw what few pence they had at both organisations in the secure knowledge that when a new school gabardine coat was needed, one or the other would provide it. It really was as simple as that.

I can recall many times, especially in the weeks before Christmas, being in friends' houses when the SVP would call with an envelope or a hamper. Once, I was at Mass with one of those friends on the day after the SVP had called, and I saw her drop fifty pence into the Society's wooden box as we left the church. So it was never really about charity; it was about investing in our community and in our own future. It was about looking after the whole parish because we never knew when ours would be the family in need of the hamper, the envelope, or even just the knock on the door. This wasn't Live Aid; this was like a very crude pension plan. It wasn't selflessness; it was self-preservation.

I remember, back then, somebody in religion class in school asking a teacher about the saint who lent his name to the SVP. What did she know about him, the student wanted to know. In those days before Wikipedia, the teacher admitted that she didn't know anything at all about who Vincent de Paul was or where he came from. At the click of a mouse, I can now tell that enquirer that Vincent was a French priest who performed many charitable works, but what fascinated me back then was that it hadn't occurred to any of us that Vincent de Paul might ever have been a real person. The society was such a cornerstone of our lives, of our local community, that it seemed almost ridiculous to think of it as anything other than a living, breathing collection of selfless individuals who quietly and without fuss appeared on your porch when times became too hard. Even now, as an adult poking around the internet, I find it odd to imagine Frédéric Ozanam, who founded the Society in France in 1833, moving amongst the Parisian poor of the nineteenth century. To me, that is not what the SVP is. To me, simply, the SVP is help. When I was a child in the 1980s, it was help in Greenhills. Now, it is help in a different part of Dublin but still always help. Right here, right now.

As time went on and I moved with it, the SVP has always remained a sort of one-stop shop where funds and goods could be deposited and goodwill stored up, ahead of any possible future calamity. When we bought our first home in London, we gave some of the previous owners' furniture to the local SVP organisation – less visible in our solidly middle-class borough than they had been back in Greenhills – but nonetheless grateful for our fridge and cooker, which they told us would go into nearby flats they were furnishing for men who had spent time living rough on the streets. 'Many of them are Irish,' the (English) SVP volunteer told me, which again made the work of the organisation – even in a foreign country – seem entirely local. Charity might begin at home, but even when you're far away, it can still watch over you.

When we moved back to Ireland, as gloom turned to boom, I would see the organisation in action again. On a freezing day in November, a family from Pakistan moved into a rented house on our road. They had four children who, as far as I could tell from their first tentative forays into forming friendships with my own kids, only possessed the – very beautiful – clothes they stood in. As an Irish winter wrapped around them, I did the only thing I knew to do – I contacted the St Vincent de Paul. Within days, all four children had brand-new, fleece-lined anoraks and solid runners had replaced their flimsy sandals. That Christmas, these new arrivals had their first SVP hamper. 'We don't celebrate Christmas,' the children's delighted mother told me, 'but this we are keeping.'

But of course those were the good times, when the haves didn't just outnumber the have nots – they almost rendered them invisible in an increasingly affluent Ireland. And with a lighter caseload and a seemingly endless stream of donations, it was a good time for the Society as well. I did an interview for the *Sunday Tribune* with an officer from the SVP just ahead of Christmas, at the very height of the boom. He told me times were good, that donations were flying, and that everyone on the organisation's books would be well looked-after that Christmas. He confided that some of the children under their care were looking for Playstations from Santa, and that he wouldn't be at all surprised if they got them. It's difficult to believe now that that was only a few years ago. It's difficult to believe how everything could change so quickly, and so catastrophically.

But it did. And once again, the SVP stepped up to the plate. More than government ministers, more than anonymous bankers, more than any of the stern-faced officials from the IMF, the members of the St Vincent de Paul were the people who witnessed – and continue to witness – at first hand the effect that boom and bust has had on the ordinary people of Ireland. Earlier this year, through a volunteer in Munster, I heard a truly shocking story of a family living just outside a small rural town, whose newly built home had stood as a testament to their good fortune during the Celtic Tiger era. From the road, the house looked rich and splendid, with a substantial wooden deck behind it overlooking some suitably postcard-perfect rolling scenery. When the family finally called on the SVP for help, the volunteers found that the children's bedrooms had been stripped of their floorboards, which their father had been burning in the fireplace in an effort to keep his young family warm. Asked why he hadn't burnt the deck instead, the father conceded that it was because he didn't want people driving past the house to see just how diminished the family's living conditions were.

That is what the St Vincent de Paul Society deals with every day in this new, reduced Ireland. They don't just engage in the practicalities of arranging a fill of heating oil and restocking empty kitchen cupboards; they also bear the responsibility for people's mental well-being, for restoring their sense of dignity and self-respect. They do so through their discretion, their kindness, their simple presence. They don't just bring peat briquettes and food, they bring a reminder that poverty is merely a symptom of a malaise in society – it is not, in itself, either an illness or an occasion of shame. The SVP fills bellies and warms houses, but its volunteers also try to lift heads and spirits, and restore a sense of self-worth to the people it helps – a massive challenge in a country that has been brought to its knees, and one which rightly makes the volunteers of the SVP the quietest, littlest-sung heroes in every town and village in the country.

There are more than 10,000 of those volunteers now, dealing with the thousands of calls that come daily to the

Society's regional offices. With no palpable sign of economic recovery on the horizon, demands on the SVP's services and resources continue to escalate. In 2011, in just four regional offices, calls were up by almost 50 per cent, while the Society estimates an increase in the order of 83 per cent in calls since 2009. Currently, one in four applications to the Society for assistance are coming from people who have never contacted the SVP before. At a time when we are bombarded with news headlines about billions, bailouts and bondholders, that is the more tangible reality of life in post-boom Ireland at the start of the twenty-first century.

Unfortunately, the Society's work is never done. Nor can any of us – who dutifully push our couple of euro into their wooden boxes once a month or who click the 'donate' button online – know for sure that we will never need the services of the St Vincent de Paul. In my own case, at least, that's why I continue to contribute to the Society. Simply put, we know not the day nor the hour. But we do know that if it does come, the SVP will be there for us.

And maybe that's why it doesn't feel like donating to a charity. Rather, it is a deposit on a hamper, a down payment against an uncertain future. And always, it is an endorsement of the amazing work done by the tireless men and women of the St Vincent de Paul, who, in an increasingly globalised society, remind us all of the importance of supporting our local community.

Across the world, the SVP now offers assistance to the poor and the needy in 132 countries. Just as in Ireland, their work, primarily through home visits, is all about the community, the neighbourhood, the local. Globally, locally, it is a bunch of extraordinary volunteers committed to performing ordinary acts of kindness. It is not about headline grabbing or scene stealing; the SVP is neither fashionable nor glamorous. Because, ultimately, being unable to heat your home is not glamorous; feeling desperately worthless because you cannot feed your children is not fashionable. But it is very, very real. With all due respect to a 400-year-old priest from France, the very fact that when we say his name we think not of him but of our friends and neighbours whose welfare depends on volunteers working in his name speaks volumes for the important work the Society continues to do. St Vincent de Paul? Real. Here. Now.

Fiona Looney is a writer, broadcaster and mother of three living in Dublin.

Editor's Introduction

Bill Lawlor

The Society of St Vincent de Paul (SVP) is among the best known of Ireland's charities. There is widespread awareness of the work of the organisation in helping those in need and this information is constantly updated via print and social media.

Up to now, however, no single-volume publication has detailed the origins, structure, administration and institutions of the SVP, as well as its work for the less well-off and socially deprived in the community. This book aims to fill that vacuum by outlining how the Society established vital amenities to facilitate its caring philosophy and highlighting its efforts to ease the plight of the disadvantaged through day-to-day support and friendship.

These include visiting the homes of those who call upon the organisation for help; meeting people in hospitals and prisons; providing financial support; running breakfast and homework clubs for school-going children in disadvantaged communities, in addition to preschools and crèches. It is also the single biggest provider of hostel and social housing accommodation in Ireland.

The society also supplies advice, counselling and a budgeting service, and is involved in running youth clubs and family resource centres. Financial aid for education is of high priority, while the provision of short holiday breaks for older people, families, children and young people has been a much-appreciated area of activity over many years.

The society's clothing and house goods shops are a familiar sight throughout Ireland and the funds generated contribute enormously to local SVP efforts in assisting the needy. These activities are among the subjects covered in the pages of this book.

Established on Charles Street, Dublin, on 16 December 1844, the Society of Saint Vincent de Paul grew rapidly, fuelled as it was by the horrors of the Famine. Expansion was such that, by the end of 1845, five Conferences (local groups) were active in Dublin city. The following year, Conferences were started in Cork, Limerick, Kerry and Waterford. A Belfast Conference was formed in 1850. Today there are 1,235 Conferences in Ireland with 10,500 members and 1,500 auxiliary members.

While women now play a major role in the Society, and account for a huge proportion of its membership, it was not until 1962 that the first women's branches were established in Galway and Ballina.

Its basic structure has remained largely unchanged since the beginning. A Conference is still the primary building block of the organisation. It is comprised of a group of people who meet as Vincentian members in a parish. An area council is made up of all the Conference presidents in a particular geographic locality. Area council presidents meet regularly at regional council meetings. Regional presidents and other members with particular responsibilities within the Society form the SVP's National Council of Ireland, which has its headquarters at SVP House, Sean McDermott Street, Dublin 1.

The cornerstone of the SVP's work is still the provision of help to those who seek it, regardless of creed, opinion, colour, age, social or economic status, gender or ethnic origin.

It is in that spirit that this now global charity looks to the future, confident and prepared to render its assistance, if called upon, to the most disadvantaged in society.

Bill Lawlor, Editor
September 2014

Historical Accounts of the Society of St Vincent de Paul

The Society of Saint Vincent de Paul: The Early History

Gerry Martin

*P*icture a quiet Dublin street, Charles Street West, a street that had been a busy thoroughfare before Ormond Bridge was rebuilt, which diverted the traffic to the new Chancery Place. It was not, however, without its inhabitants, and the traders in iron products and small public houses were many, backed by the tenement dwellings of the poor. Thomas Willis (1790–1881), an apothecary who occupied 34 Upper Ormond Quay just around the corner, had carried out a survey of the inhabitants of the parish of St Michan's. This inquiry, entitled 'Facts Connected with the Social and Sanitary Conditions of the Working Classes in the City of Dublin', concerned itself with the living conditions of the parish residents. The report into the overcrowding, the absence of water for the most basic kind of washing, the diseases, amongst other issues, was to create a great deal of concern, which led – sixty years later – to the redevelopment of the area. The northside market was replaced in the last days of the nineteenth century by the present St Michan's Street (Fisher's Lane) and this resulted in the clearance

3

of one of the most congested districts in Dublin. In this parish was Newgate Prison, which had been transferred from the city walls in 1773 to Green Street, now probably better known for its courthouse. Here, several of the United Irishmen were imprisoned – and executed – in 1798; in 1848, it held John Mitchel and other members of the Young Ireland party. Mitchel was a good friend of John O'Hagan of the Society of St Vincent de Paul (see below).

Thomas Willis's study was particularly concerned with the impact of his words. He wrote as an introduction: 'In placing before the public the result of some inquiries amongst the working classes, I am fully sensible of the risk I incur, in making statements of such a startling nature as to appear incredible to those whose attention has never been directed to such matters.'[1]

Willis was one of seven men, including two clergymen, who sat down at the White Cross Rooms at 8.30 p.m. on Monday, 16 December 1844 to plan the introduction of the French Society of St Vincent de Paul to Ireland. They would establish five branches throughout the city during the following year.

Willis was a very influential member of the Society of St Vincent de Paul. His work and that of his colleagues and their concerns set the agenda for the Society's endeavours for the next 168 years. There was an emphasis on giving aid, but an equal emphasis was placed on calling for an improvement in living conditions for all, for better housing, for an adequate welfare system. This remains the Society's aim today.

Willis was additionally to be a Guardian of the Poor Law in Dublin North (Brunswick Street) until he was sent

---

1   Thomas Willis, *Facts Connected with the Social and Sanitary Conditions of the Working Classes in the City of Dublin* (Dublin, 1845), p. iii.

down to Bantry, Co. Cork, as a medical inspector during the Great Famine. During his time in Bantry, he was given credit for the invention of the hinged or sliding coffin, later made into crosses and presented to various convents: 'During the frightful famine plague which devastated a large proportion of Ireland in the years 1846–47 that monstrous and unchristian machine, a "sliding coffin" was from necessity used in Bantry Union for the conveyance of the victims to one common grave. The material of this Cross, the symbol of our Redemption, is a portion of one of the machines which enclosed the remains of several hundred of our countrymen during their passage from their wretched huts or the wayside where they died to the pit into which their remains were thrown.'[2]

Willis was a colourful character, his personal appearance being striking, as a description of the time records: 'The old medico who wore the broad-brimmed hat of a bishop and the white cravat of a Brummel was a familiar figure in Dublin from the days of George the Third. The favourite post of Dr Willis was at book sales or by the bed-side of the sick poor.'

Willis's premises, the White Cross Rooms, were leased to the Religious Society of Friends (Quakers) during the Famine to provide a soup kitchen for those affected. The lease has signatures of well-known names such as Joseph Bewley and Jonathan Pim. Even earlier, the district was the original base for the Sick & Indigent Roomkeepers Society, which had a life in adjoining Mountrath Street.

The Poor Law (Ireland) Act had no doubt stirred those men with a social conscience into action. The Poor Law Amendment Act in Britain had exercised minds since 1834, and efforts were in place to make Paris into Prefect Claude

---

2   P. Hickey, *Cork Examiner*, 24 March 1989.

de Rambuteau's ideal of a disease-free city – 20,000 people had died in the cholera epidemic of 1832, just twelve months before the French society was founded. The 1838 Irish Act decreed that relief was only available within a workhouse – unlike the equivalent English Act, which allowed outdoor relief to the poor.

The workhouse was to be a crude solution. On the other hand, we are told by R.B. McDowell that, before the Famine, the first Poor Law Commissioners saw it differently: 'The poor-law system, they were convinced, was bound to play a mighty part in inaugurating a new era in public life, when the prevalence of official impartiality, efficiency, economy and standardised and scientific methods of administration would raise the moral tone of the whole community.'[3]

The *Freeman's Journal,* in a hard-hitting article, had said that it was well known that they were not 'enamoured' by the Poor Law: 'We have been always of opinion that they were calculated to superadd discontent to misery and to excite wretchedness to outrage, by the exhibition of sleek and well-paid officials, pampered upon the hard-wrung farthings of the poor.'

The newspaper went on to work out the cost per head of the Poor Law for each pauper in the land.[4] This gave the Society of St Vincent de Paul its lead. They could cut down bureaucracy through the use of volunteers. They could and would help the many people who, through no fault of their own, were without resources. That was the plan – in many cases it was abandoned, but in many cases, such as in Cork during the Famine, it was a triumph.

Daniel O'Connell died in Italy in 1847, at the age of seventy-one. Despite his charitable record, there is no

---

3   R.B. McDowell, 'Ireland on the eve of the Famine' in Virginia Crossman, *Local Government in Nineteenth-century Ireland* (Belfast, 1994), p.47.
4   *Freeman's Journal*, 15 December 1843.

evidence that he aided the Society, but his son John is recorded in the first SVP minute book as having been a member (although most likely an 'honorary' member). However, many of the Vincentians had an alternative view to that of The Liberator. They were from the ranks of Young Ireland. Called the 'quasi-rebels' by John Henry Newman, John O'Hagan, the poet and barrister, and Richard D'Alton Williams, the doctor, were but two of these 'agitators'.

Another man with a conscience, though not known as a Vincentian, was Frederick Lucas, the well-known editor of the *Tablet*. He wrote several articles on charity and described the desperate conditions of the poor. He also referred specifically to the apathy of the State with regard to these poor, and also the apathy of influential Catholics, who could have done much more: 'Who except the clergy visit the poor? As far as we laity are concerned, the approved plan seems to be to manage all by a secretary, to avoid all dirty work whenever it can be avoided and to labour by a committee; or we try to do charity by nothing as vulgar as the sweat of the brow, in which all must labour, but by polite, genteel, not over strained exertion of ladies and gentlemen in white kid gloves. We have already endeavoured to introduce to the favour of our readers a French society for lay persons. We refer to the Society of St Vincent de Paul.' [5]

Frederick Lucas regarded the youthful nature of the original Paris Conference as 'an accident or more truly a Providence,' and recites the international society's report regarding the advantages of youthful membership as valuable training: 'The Society of St Vincent de Paul habituates us early in life to the practice of Charity. It thus prepares a generation of men who will have learned, at

---

5   Frederick Lucas, *Paris Archive SVP* (Article of English & Wales Society, 1994).

the age of generous dispositions, to see in the world other things besides themselves; who will have taken a sufficiently near view of the miseries of humanity, to be able to apply a remedy when the time comes for them also to occupy a responsible position in the world.'[6]

Lucas had been at the initial meeting of the SVP in London, which also happened in 1844, and had been offered the presidency of the English society. He declined the honour. Lucas brought the *Tablet* to Dublin in 1849, and he became a Member of Parliament.

The Irish SVP was formed only fifteen years after the Catholic Emancipation Act. There was an element of emulation of the main Protestant charities, such as the Association for the Relief of Distressed Protestants (ARDP), but when the Poor Law rate was introduced in 1838, there was a feeling amongst the members of the established church that voluntary charity alms-giving was then 'a thing of the past.' However, post-Emancipation, middle-class Catholics were intent on mirroring the social concerns – and ambitions – of their Protestant friends and neighbours.

Little is known of the first president of the Society, Redmund Peter O'Carroll (1804–1847), although a brief account of his earlier life is told in Burke's *Vicissitudes of Families*.[7] He was a married man, aged forty, much older than most of the other initial members. He lived on Great Charles Street, off Mountjoy Square, in a substantial house with his wife and two sons. The sons were later to join the priesthood; one, who joined the Jesuits, had a distinguished career. That son was a professor of modern languages at the Royal College in Dublin and was reputed to speak fourteen

---

6   *The Tablet*, 27 January 1844.
7   Bernard Burke, *Vicissitudes of Families* (London, 1883).

languages fluently. He also wrote extensively for the *Gaelic Journal*, the forerunner for Gaelic League publications.

Redmund O'Carroll was initially law advisor to the Commissioners of National Education. He was then appointed Catholic secretary to the Charitable Bequests Board, at a time when there was difficulty with both Roman Catholic and Protestant bishops when it came to the proper beneficiary of a will. He also formed a friendship with Archbishop Denis Affre of Paris, who was killed on the barricades in his city in 1848. Affre assembled a committee in 1847 to send money to Ireland for the Great Famine, and it was to Dr Daniel Murray, Archbishop of Dublin, and to O'Carroll, that he directed the funds, for O'Carroll was to be the Irish link in distribution. (In a letter dated 27 May 1847, O'Carroll was able to tell Archbishop Murray that the sum of £6,000 had been sent to the Society in Ireland by the international society.)[8]

O'Carroll, who attended the first meeting of the Society of St Vincent de Paul in the White Cross Rooms, went out to Bray, Co. Wicklow regularly, and there is a warm letter, addressed to the Archdeacon of Dublin, inviting him to call. This letter was dated September 1847 – Redmund Peter O'Carroll was dead one month later, at the age of forty-three.[9] He is reputed to have died from typhus; whether he succumbed to this as a result of his Vincentian work we can only speculate. It was not unknown for the 'visitors' to be similarly affected when they went to the homes of fever victims.

O'Carroll's wife, Mary Catherine O'Carroll (née Goold), was governess of the Female Penitent Asylum in Dublin in 1845, and became matron of Grangegorman (Female) Prison shortly after her husband's death. The writer Maria

---

8   DDA, Murray Papers, 27 May 1847.
9   *Ibid.*, 3 September 1847.

Luddy tells us that the 'exclusive use of this prison for women was an innovative and unprecedented step' in penal history in these islands.[10] That Mrs O'Carroll was also a correspondent of Very Rev. Dr Murray is evidenced by a letter, in French, to the Archbishop, dated June 1847, where she refers to a death in her family, 'and other matters'; her husband and children join her 'in sending good wishes' to the Archbishop. [11]

Redmund knew his neighbour, Archbishop Murray (1768–1852), very well. Dr Murray was coming to the end of a long life, but he was to outlive his friend. He had a difficult life, and he was at loggerheads with some of the other members of the hierarchy on many issues, and was regarded as an unflattering 'Castle Catholic'. But he was a man of great principles and he suffered with the population during the years of famine. He had brought the Sisters of Charity, the Loreto Sisters and the Sisters of Mercy to Dublin, and it was to be complementary to a career of achievement that he saw the lay organisation of the SVP spread its wings. That it was a French society would have given him some satisfaction: 'Dr Murray ... always followed with deep interest the post-Napoleonic resurgence of the Church in France, and had much confidence in the inherent Catholicism and re-organisation fervour of the plain people of that country. It was to France rather than Italy or any other Catholic nation that he looked for practical suggestions in his task of ecclesiastical re-construction in Dublin. Many of the French Catholic forces of the time were amongst his correspondents, including Frédéric Ozanam.'[12]

10 Maria Luddy, *Women and Philanthropy in Nineteenth-century Ireland* (Cambridge, 1995), p.159.
11 DDA, *Murray Papers*, -.6.1847.
12 F.P. Carey, *Daniel Murray* (Dublin, 1938).

Redmund Peter O'Carroll, a layman, was selected as president, unusual in days of clerical influence. He was educated by the Jesuits at Stoneyhurst College in England, where Thomas Francis Meagher and other Irish nationalists had been schooled. However, there is no evidence that O'Carroll played a part in the political struggle against O'Connell. He was a barrister at the nearby Four Courts and was proficient in French – as was very necessary for one dealing with the Frenchmen of the Paris society. Regrettably, his role in the SVP was short; he was succeeded by James O'Ferrall.

We are more fortunate with another member, John O'Hagan (1822–1890). He was a poet, a barrister, and later the first judge of the Land Commission Court. O'Hagan was born in Newry, Co. Down, and was educated by the Jesuits at Hardwicke Street, Dublin, before going on to Trinity College, Dublin. We are given an account, years later, by a fellow student at the university: 'Near to me that night sat John O'Hagan. He was then not long in college and was even younger than I; so that, partially, perhaps, from a fellow-feeling, and partially for his own sake, I liked him. His appearance was open and honest, but I missed some of that firmness and strength of character which was notable in some of the others.'[13]

Aged just twenty-two years old when he was present at the first meeting, John O'Hagan is reputed to have written the first annual report of the Irish society. He was a member, and possibly a vice-president, of the Council of Ireland (Superior Council) as late as 1874. He was an intimate of Thomas Davis and Charles Gavan Duffy. O'Hagan was also proficient in French – he translated the 'Song of Roland', the poem of the Middle Ages, into English; however there is no

---

13 *United Irishman*, 21 October, 1899.

record of either O'Carroll or O'Hagan having a friendship with Frédéric Ozanam or Emmanuel 'Papa' Bailly, the first president of the international SVP. There is evidence that O'Hagan travelled to Paris to meet with Young Irelanders, such as John Mitchel, and, later, John O'Leary. There is also evidence that he defended many of his colleagues in court.

We are lucky with O'Hagan that we have a record of this significant figure both in the Society and elsewhere. His life makes an interesting observation on the nineteenth century, and his contacts – be they John Henry Newman, Anthony Trollope or William Gladstone on one hand, and John Martin, John Mitchel or John O'Leary on the other – were mixed up with his life as a Vincentian; but a Vincentian with social, if nationalist, concerns. He opined: 'It seems as if we shall soon have nothing but workhouses distributing stirabout in a country which produces twice the amount its population requires. Mechanics Institutes telling the people that their present condition is altogether the result of laziness, a National Education system teaching us Chinese, because more people speak that language than any other, and garrisons to prevent us from protesting against the whole – all presided over by the high and mighty boards most graciously appointed by ponderous charters written in a half-Saxon, half-Norman French dialect.'[14]

Very Rev. Dr Murray was to die in 1852 and was succeeded by Very Rev. Dr Paul Cullen, later to be made Cardinal Archbishop. Cullen was from the beginning suspicious of the laity and he made it clear to John O'Hagan 'that control by Catholic laymen, and by projection, an Irish state, was no more acceptable to the Irish bishops as a body.' He made a rare exception in the case of the Society of St Vincent de Paul, and James O'Ferrall and Michael Errington,

---

14 *Ibid.*

the second and third presidents, were to be included as members of various semi-religious bodies. Archbishop Cullen's views were definite and unambiguous: 'I think it is not of any great importance to have the laymen in question. They do without laymen in Belgium. We have scarcely any great laymen who could help to keep up the University and it is in the body of the people that we must reply.'[15]

Cullen had a highly selective view of the Society and it is perhaps unfortunate that his reign of thirty years coincided with the thirty years of Sir John Bradstreet, the very conservative fourth president. The society had lost some of its initial vigour, only to regain this in the twentieth century. Cardinal Cullen also had no time for the Young Ireland men, many of whom graced the ranks of the Society of St Vincent de Paul. When it came to the Catholic University, he was in a decided pickle, and he saw non-religious staff with a political leaning as being a dangerous mix.

Father Stephen Farrell, one of two priests at the first meeting, came from the Francis Street parish. He was soon joined by a group of poets and radicals – well recognised and fêted as writers, but not, perhaps, as members of a Catholic charitable organisation. John O'Hagan, Richard D'Alton Williams, Denis Florence MacCarthy and Kevin Doherty were perhaps not the only Young Irelanders to join the Society of St Vincent de Paul in its infant years – Charles Gavan Duffy is listed in July 1845, although he was probably an honorary member and subscriber. Their work was not highlighted, but in Williams's case publicly identified at his trial in 1848. Gavan Duffy's own commitment to the poor, while not evidenced in the annals of the Society, is recorded in the letters of Dr

---

15 Emmet Larkin, *The Consolidation of the Roman Catholic Church in Ireland, 1860-1870* (Dublin, 1987), p. 169.

Blake, Bishop of Dromore, who wrote to him in 1849:
'… what especially delights me is your resolution to make
your leisure time subservient to the great purpose of
providing immediate relief for our starving and perishing
people.'[16]

By 1849 Gavan Duffy was negotiating for the revival
of the *Nation* and had re-established his weekly suppers
– although his friend John O'Hagan, then a successful
barrister, only joined them occasionally. A newcomer
amongst the guests was George Waters, a county court
judge, who was later to be the fifth president of the Society
of St Vincent de Paul.[17] O'Hagan and Denis MacCarthy
were good friends and the youthful humour of the young
members of the Society is perhaps brought out by a
comment made by Rev. Matthew Russell S.J. describing
the young rebels as daily Mass attenders, 'following which
they proceeded to the country to concoct Lord knows what
treason.'[18] Russell is pleased to remind us of MacCarthy's
gleeful response: 'So you have heard of our Sunday prayers
and peripatetics – here is a change with a vengeance – getting
pious and constitutional at the one moment! … while in
the Haddington Road Chapel we are exoterically saying our
prayers, we are esoterically appealing to the masses.'[19]

To instance the close friendships that existed between
these men it can be noted that, just before the first
meeting, O'Hagan, MacCarthy and Gavan Duffy had
taken a holiday touring the south of the country. They
finished at Derrynane, Co. Kerry, the family home of
Daniel and John O'Connell. Then, twelve months later
– immediately after the Society's first general meeting

---

16 C.G. Duffy, *My Life in Two Hemispheres*, Vol. 2 (London, 1898), p.81.
17 *Ibid.*, p.14.
18 Rev. M. Russell S.J., *Irish Monthly*, 1903, pp. 8-9.
19 *Ibid.*

in July 1845 – O'Hagan, Duffy, John Martin and John Mitchel went on holiday to Donegal.[20]

The third poet, Richard D'Alton Williams (1822-1862) was, at the time that he joined the Society, a medical student at St Vincent's Hospital. He was born in Dublin, but with the death of his father and the subsequent remarriage of his mother he had been brought up in Toomevara, Co. Tipperary, at the home of his stepfather, Count D'Alton. In 1835, young Richard was sent to be educated at the Jesuit College of St Stanislaus at Tullabeg, Co. Offaly (King's County), where the prefect of studies was Fr. Meagher, uncle of Thomas Francis Meagher, another Young Irelander. Following some years spent at the college in Carlow, Williams moved to Dublin in 1843 to pursue his medical studies. That same year he had his 'Munster War Song' published in the *Nation*, under the pen name of 'Shamrock'. Subsequent involvement with Kevin Izod Doherty in the short-lived *Irish Tribune* led to Williams's arrest on a charge of treason-felony, but an acquittal followed, the above-mentioned John O'Hagan being part of his legal team of lawyers. Williams was to subsequently qualify in Edinburgh as a doctor, and later to emigrate to America, where he died in 1862, aged forty.

Rev. Russell, narrating the involvement of Richard in the work of the Society, tells of records ' ... from musty archives [including] a quarto containing the visiting tickets, filled up by the members of the Vincent de Paul Society, thirty years ago.' Amongst these, 'as clear as if written yesterday, were many entries signed by R.D. Williams alone, and some by Williams and D.F. MacCarthy together.' Russell quotes from a number of 'tickets', dated Saturday, 16 January 1847, where the visitors had written: 'The annals of our Society can

---

20 J. O'Hagan, 'Ulster in the Summer of 1845', *Irish Monthly*, 1913.

furnish few instances of greater misery than this. Friendless, landless, penniless, without food, without health, without hope, the wretched families, sick and shivering, starves in a corner, while their father is vainly looking for employment, and the miserable, half-clad mother – herself requiring at least repose, for she is pregnant – the daily less and less able to oppose the strength of maternal instincts to the onset of disease. Besides the fullest allowance of bread, meal and soup, we think the Society might reasonably advance some money to redeem pledged clothes and pay the rent (one shilling a week) for those utterly destitute outcasts.'[21]

It was the Catholic University that created a rather difficult scenario for the Church in Ireland. John Henry Newman had been appointed to act as first rector and John O'Hagan had been appointed to lecture on personal economics. Newman and O'Hagan became firm friends, a friendship which carried on to Newman's death. The Irishman wrote to the Englishman in lamentable terms on the latter's decision to leave Dublin; however, they collaborated fruitfully in the journals the *Rambler* and the *Atlantis*. Newman was followed as rector by Rev. Bartholomew Woodlock (1819–1902), a well-connected priest who was the first spiritual director of the Society of St Vincent de Paul and who had been at the first meeting in December 1844. He became Bishop of Ardagh and Clonmacnoise, and was reputed to have remained an adviser to the local Conference in Longford until his resignation as bishop.

Woodlock, with relatives such as Bartholomew Teeling of 1798 fame, Francis Sylvester Mahony ('Fr. Prout') and Sir Dominic Corrigan, MP, cannot have been immune to the rebellious atmosphere of the time, but we know nothing

21 M.R., 'Relics of Richard D'Alton Williams', in the *Irish Monthly*, 1877, pp. 332-7.

of his views on social and political issues – nor those of the other clerical founder (already mentioned), Fr. Stephen Anster Farrell (1806–1879). The latter was instrumental in setting up one of the early Conferences (branches) at Francis Street in Dublin. He was educated at Trinity College, although born in Cork where his father, Martin Farrell, had been a schoolmaster and also an active member of the Cork Charitable Society. Young Stephen carried the name of his mother, Anster, made renowned by his cousin, the poet John Martin Anster (1793-1867), whose principal notoriety was as composer of a prizewinning essay on the death of Princess Charlotte of Wales, and more especially as the translator of Goethe's *Faust*, the first rendering into English of any part of that work. He was said also to be a founder of *Dublin University Magazine*.

Rev. Woodlock was a disparate character. As stated, he was president of All Hallows College in Dublin, the second rector – after John Henry Newman – of the Catholic University, vicar general to Paul Cullen, and, eventually, Bishop of Ardagh and Clonmacnoise. He was a loyal priest, even when things became thorny with the university and with Cardinal Cullen. In fact it must have been a relief to reach the height of the bishopric.

As with the earlier members of the Society, O'Carroll, O'Hagan, O'Ferrall, Errington and Bradstreet left no living descendants. O'Hagan and Bradstreet were childless, O'Carroll had two sons, both priests, and Errington had a son, George, who became a well-known MP, but was childless. It is as though high office had robbed them of family. Their work was demanding; they had a 'mission'.

The 'vocation of the laity' was not a concept that would have been readily understood in 1844, many years before Vatican I – never mind Vatican II – but it was an era of altruism, when denominational charity was the norm. The lay character of the organisation was clear, although the spiritual aspect of the work was also evident. The laymen who comprised the first 'Brothers' would not have previously been too closely identified with the poor families they visited, for the visitors represented a new Catholic establishment. These men – women were not admitted to the ranks until a century later – led a comfortable existence and this added to the unlikely nature of their direct contact with the poor.

Dublin's *Nation* newspaper, in reviewing *A Christmas Carol* in 1844, set the tone of the time, and suggested that: 'Charles Dickens looks upon England, and he sees niggardly wealth and menacing poverty side by side, casting squints at each other, which promises battles.'[22]

Rather than casting sideways glances, the early members of the Society took an alternative view of communication. 'Person-to-person contact' had been the emphasis of the new brotherhood, and visiting the destitute in the Dickensian conditions of 1844 Dublin must have required an unusual sense of concern and a special awareness of poverty for people brought up in privileged conditions. The person-to-person contact represented a strategy which lives on to this day, and weekly visits to family homes is the norm for the Society. That this was later extended to prison and hospital visitation was a recognition that 'home' was a transferable location, and, indeed, subsequent work in orphanages meant the provision of homes for youngsters deprived of family life. Educational provision followed as a natural consequence.

In the Ireland of today, poverty may have changed its name to 'exclusion', but the role of the Society would still be recognised by those men whose names are contained in the first minute book.

---

22 *Nation*, 6th January 1844

If the foundation in Paris in 1833 was the consequence of a defence of Christianity, the undertaking in Dublin was clearly seen in more temporal terms as the natural extension, to Ireland, of an established organisation. The structure of an international fraternity was already in place, and formal rules and objectives had been adopted and recognised. The Christian ethos of the Society was unquestioned and was reflected in these rules – 'self-sanctification' being understood as the prime objective – and the work of the movement had been dedicated to St Vincent de Paul, whose patronage had been claimed by many nineteenth-century foundations and who had been recognised by the Roman Catholic Church as the patron of all charitable works. However, if the *spirit* of St Vincent was accepted as a motivating force, did 'spirituality' appear as an outward motivation for the early members in Ireland?[23]

A twentieth-century writer describes the Catholic laity as being 'passive' in the matter of evangelisation, happy to leave the role of the evangeliser to the ordained, and there is such passivity discernible in the absence of references to the spiritual needs of both members and 'cases' in the early minutes.[24] One must speculate that the lay members saw 'religion' as the province of the priests, and the early introduction of 'spiritual advisers' to Irish Conferences would suggest that this was so – leaving the 'social work' of the Society to the laity.

The acceptance of this situation by both clergy and laity was taken for granted, which may account for the limited roles of Frs. Woodlock and Farrell, and their appearance as remote figures. There is clearly no evidence that either priest interfered with the laity's relief agenda. Did this represent a contemporary compartmentalisation of functions amongst

---

23 SVP (Irish) Minutes, 21 July 1845.
24 Susan W. Blum, *The Ministry of Evangelization* (Minnesota, 1988), p. 19.

the Roman Catholic faithful, not practised in the charitable organisations of the Established Church, such as ARDP, where, significantly, the clergy played a more intrusive role?

Frédéric Ozanam criticised a new Conference of the Society on one occasion when the members enquired about the records of other, earlier Conferences; they sought the precedents of earlier days to guide their actions. Ozanam retorted that such documents had been lost, but in any event this 'summery of our work contained, perhaps, a note of pride.'[25] In essence, the members should look to the future and not be hostages to the ways other members had performed. Despite this call for humility, the note of pride is still evident in the number of subsequent publications that have been issued, which aspire to be true narrations of the origins of the French society. However, the absence of minutes of the early meetings has presented a vacuum that various authors have addressed in different fashions.

Ozanam, of course, was prepared to put down on paper his thoughts – about the young society, about being a Christian, about being a Vincentian – and we are fortunate to have most of these writings available to us in good translations.

This is a similar note of the same pride!

---

25   C.K. Murphy, *The Spirit of the Society of St. Vincent de Paul* (Dublin, 1944), p.27

The Society of St Vincent De Paul in Cork, 1846-1946: One Hundred Years of Charity

Bill Lawlor

A sermon by a Passionist priest in 1846 is reckoned to have led to the establishment of the Society of St Vincent de Paul in Cork. Its formation is said to have followed the suggestion in the course of a homily by the Very Rev. Bartholomew Russell, OP of St Mary's in the city.

The information comes to light in a rare local SVP booklet, *One Hundred Years of Charity, 1846–1946*, which records that the historic occurrence was referred to at the 1890 quarterly general meeting of the Society's Council of Cork, which also mentioned the death of Father Russell.

Details on the early years are scarce, as the first minute book of the Society is lost and the minutes of 1861 'begin tantalisingly with the number 666', says the booklet. The devil may be in the detail, as the publication adds, 'we can only surmise what is contained in the 665 sheets now lost to us.' The missing records cover the first fifteen years of the work of the Society in Cork, including the Famine period and the formation of the first three Conferences, as well as the names of those who founded the organisation in Cork.

By 1946 there were thirty-one Conferences, ten of them involved in special works. These followed the formation of the Conferences of St Patrick's in 1877, and St Vincent's in 1912. In the next thirty years, sixteen Conferences and ten special works were established – an average of almost one foundation a year. Conferences set up within that period included UCG (1919) and Cork Catholic Young Men's Society (1932).

Home Visitation

In many ways the problems confronting society in Cork in the Famine era of the 1840s reflect those of today's austerity, where so many individuals and families, including children, face constant hunger and deprivation as the economic crisis drags on.

This is particularly evident in the SVP's central work of home visitation, which ensures that the basic necessities of food, heat and clothing are provided for. The centenary booklet relates that, 'since March 1846 there has not passed a single week in which members, Cork citizens, have not sought out their fellow Christians in their poor homes.'

It says that a reference to the Famine years in a minute of thirty years later shows that the expenditure of the Society in 1848 was five times higher than that of 1846.

The largest number of families ever visited in a single month, and the largest sum ever spent on their relief in the same period prior to the years 1930–1932, is that of February 1880, when 905 families were assisted at an expenditure of £797. In the whole of that year, 3,327 families were relieved at an expenditure of £4,190, of which £1,400 was subscribed by the Cork Relief Fund. This was an emergency organisation formed for the express purpose of helping the Society through a period of grave depression.

However, it was the depression years of the early 1930s that saw unprecedented demands upon the Society in Cork. From 1930–1932, the entire annual income of the Society was consumed in dealing with the distress of hungry families and individuals.

The troubled times in Ireland, not surprisingly, brought problems for the SVP, but reports show that, 'notwithstanding the inconvenience of the curfews, 1920–1921, there was no interruption of Conference meetings or of the visitation of the poor, though both had to be carried out under extreme difficulties.'

There were other risks associated with visitation in those times when contagious disease was widespread. However, the dangers were unhesitatingly faced by the volunteers.

Among the perils was smallpox and the *Cork Examiner* of June 1872 contains a letter from the Society appealing for funds for the relief of sufferers. But even as late as the 1940s, the SVP in the southern city was averaging 700–900 home visits each week, or 120–150 a day.

Dockers' Hostel

It is one of the finest natural harbours in the world and has always been an important industrial area, while the beauty of its seascapes has made it a top recreational and tourist venue. So, not surprisingly, during the early years of the twentieth century, the Port of Cork was even then a hive of activity, especially commercial, where men gathered in search of scarce work opportunities.

Its scenic charm, however, did nothing to ease the conditions of labourers who clamoured for employment on the quayside. These were often harsh and uncompromising.

It is in this context that the practical assistance and concern of St Vincent de Paul proved hugely beneficial in easing the plight of dockers.

According to *One Hundred Years of Charity, 1846-1946*, during the World War I and before hours of employment in the docks were regulated, men often waited on the quays all through the night for the arrival of an expected vessel.

To mitigate the extreme hardship of these circumstances, especially in severe weather, the Society opened a hostel for dockers on Parnell Place, 'where men might await in warmth and comfort the arrival of a ship, and in the interval take their meals.' It records that once, on a single day, as many as 900 men availed themselves of the facilities offered by this accommodation.

At that time, the International Organisation of the Apostleship of the Sea operated through the Society. The Cork Council of the Society was a recognised unit of the apostleship. It had the duty of visiting ships, calling to the port and assisting seamen to attend Mass and receive the sacraments. It also supplied them with objects of piety and reading, and offered whatever other services it could.

Refuge for the Homeless

Providing a place of refuge for the homeless has always been a priority for the Society. To deal with this particular need in Cork, a large house on Merchant's Quay was purchased and converted to a hostel capable of accommodating seventy men.

St Vincent's Hostel opened in October 1933 and sheltered thirty-four men initially, but this figure soon grew to seventy-one. One of its most important features was its oratory, which remained functional despite pressure for the provision of extra space.

The *100 Years of Charity* document states: 'The hostel may be said most fully to show forth the two essential functions of every true work of the Society of St. Vincent de Paul: that from it radiate spiritual and material charity.'

The hostel project was followed by the establishment of a club for the homeless in Queen Street, availed of by up to 100 men a day. This large hall saw the serving of penny suppers each night, while the Cork Penny Dinners Committee provided a similar meal, thereby ensuring that an unemployed man could have at least two good meals a day for two pence.

Concern for the Sick

The needs of the sick, whether financial or in the activity of visitation, have consistently been of primary importance to the Society. In the 1930s and 1940s and indeed before, those who fell seriously ill experienced major financial problems in the absence of suitable welfare benefits. The society was also concerned about consequential hardships for these people left to fend for themselves.

The booklet states that the local Conferences were 'indebted to many city doctors for their professional services generously rendered.' It goes on, 'The sick of the District Hospital are visited each week. Though all their material wants are supplied, the loneliness and isolation due to separation from relatives and friends by distance or by death can weight heavily upon hospital patients.'

Wardrobes of the Poor

Long before the establishment of today's nationwide SVP Vincent's shops, which are an extremely valuable resource in providing clothing for the less well-off as well as a fundraising mechanism through sales to bargain seekers, the Society kept the 'wardrobes of the poor'.

Obliged by its own rule to do so, it kept the wardrobes full, the source of supply being largely the charity of the Christian community.

In the twentieth century, up to 1946, the Society in Cork clothed the poor with mostly cast-off garments. The booklet says it had 'great help from many ladies of the city' who devoted themselves to the work. Referring to the stress of circumstances associated with World War II, it states a new and more exhaustive system of clothes collection was found to be necessary: 'The collection is now systematically made throughout the entire city and suburbs. Much of its immediate success is attributable to the fact that it was introduced to the public by his Lordship, the Bishop of Cork, who initiated the appeal.' It goes on, 'The society is indebted to city manufacturers who added of their great generosity large quantities of new articles to supply the unavoidable deficiencies of a collection of cast-off clothes.'

The Importance of Youth Membership

Early records show that at one time senior members of the Society associated their sons with the organisation through the payment of an annual subscription. Later, the boy, 'though scarcely yet a young man,' would be introduced to the Society. The records reveal the uninterrupted connection of families in Cork with the Society through three or four generations stretching back to 1846.

Organised work for youth within the Conferences led to the formation of dedicated Conferences in the schools and Cork University. The double advantage of the changing personnel of a students' Conference is remarked upon: 'It brings many into the Society and almost invariably leads to

26

the formation of new Conferences to retain and hold those who have passed from the school.'

The booklet also records: "'The Presentation Brothers" College has been a prolific source of energy and zeal. The first contact of the Society was made with it a number of years ago. An excellent students' Conference was founded. With the passing of time a second Conference composed of past pupils was established.'

Some years later, a Conference of past pupils of the Christian Brothers College was formed.

Cork SVP's Role in Education

The society played a significant role in the provision of adult education in Cork. In 1864 the SVP founded its first night school in St Finnbarr's parish. Shortly after, schools were opened in the Cathedral Parish and Blackpool. The schools were an immediate success: in November 1867, no less than 300 boys were attending the St Finnbarr Parish Schools.

St Finnbarr's Schools were housed in the South Presentation Monastery by permission of the Brothers of the community. The North Parish Schools were originally carried on in a house in the district and later in a room in the Blarney Street Schools.

The subjects taught were religion, reading, writing, arithmetic and bookkeeping. During the day, the majority of the boys were employed as shop porters, while others were among the employees of the Flax Factory.

Says the booklet: 'Whenever the reports discuss the need of the schools it is invariably to say that the children and boys are prevented from attending day schools because they are at work in the factories and warehouses, or are obliged to care the house while their parents are at work.'

A report of 1878 says that one class was composed of persons whose ages ranged from twenty to thirty. The enacting of the Compulsory Education Act 1892, seems to have been the turning point in the successful life of the schools. Strenuous efforts were made by the Society to gain the recognition of school attendances by the Commissioners of National Education, but without success.

Children whose ages brought them within the provisions of the statute were obliged to withdraw from the schools. Pupils of St Finnbarr's, the last school to close, were transferred to the Boys' Brigade.

When Cork Banked on the SVP

Long before the concept of credit unions was even considered, the circumstances of the time prompted the Society to take up banking in Cork. So, in 1870, a bank was opened in SS. Peter's and Paul's Parish to 'help the poor practice thrift and guard their hard-won money.'

A second institution followed in St Finnbarr's Parish in 1873. A third bank was operating in the Cathedral Parish in 1891. The banks closed in 1915 and their accounts transferred to other institutions, including the Post Office Savings Bank.

The Welfare of Prisoners

The society's concern for the welfare of prisoners in Cork was evident in 1908, a year in which the matter 'came under consideration.' Then, in 1909, the Prisoners' Aid Society was founded. This work continued uninterrupted until 1919, when it was no longer practicable to continue it because of the political conditions that then pertained.

In 1925, however, the Prisoners' Aid Society was again reconstituted under an Irish government and continued for as long as Cork Jail was used as a prison.

SVP members visited the jail each week to talk to the inmates. Upon their release, each prisoner in need was supplied with clothing and 'assisted to his home if outside Cork'. This work ceased when Cork Jail was abandoned as a prison.

In 1940, the Borstal Institute was transferred from Clonmel to Cork. The governor invited the SVP to form a Borstal Association for collaboration with the administration in the work of the institute.

The SVP readily agreed to the proposal and 'a most exacting period of activity and service followed.' Indeed, the record shows that 'as the Society dipped deeper into borstal work its problems seemed to grow and the occasions of its usefulness to multiply.'

Visitation (at one period daily), lectures, educational classes, plays in which the boys participated, outings, games and exercise all came within the scope of the Cork society's work.

In 1943, the Society was appointed Probation Officer under the Criminal Justice Administration Act 1914. District justices subsequently put large numbers of young offenders under the care of the Society instead of committing them to Borstal, which greatly increased the workload and responsibility of the organisation in Cork.

However, in relation to that extra burden, the document states: 'Nevertheless, it has been readily assumed because of the resultant advantages to young offenders.'

Mulcahy House, Clonmel

Michael Kelly

Mulcahy House was previously Clonmel's Central Technical Institute. It became vacant in the 1960s when a new technical institute was built in the town. The Particular Council of Clonmel acquired the building from Clonmel Corporation and, with the aid of the bequest from the Patrick Mulcahy estate, it repaired and refurbished the building as headquarters for the Society in the town.

In the year 1800, a Yorkshire philanthropist initiated a series of lectures for those mechanics of Glasgow anxious to acquire information on scientific matters. The word 'mechanic' in this context referred to anyone who operated a machine. This led to the establishment of mechanics institutes throughout Britain and Ireland.

In 1845, Charles Bianconi, the mayor of Clonmel, laid the foundation stone for the Clonmel Mechanics Institute in Anglesea Street. The institute was to be for the benefit of the working classes as a means of aiding their practical skills, to direct their taste for scientific knowledge and to inspire them to invention and improvement. Three schools were established, consisting of an evening school, a day school and an art school. After the initial success, the institute gradually failed to attract those for whom it was intended.

A literary society which had sprung up within the institute took over the parent body. From 1873, it was officially known as the Clonmel Literary Institute, but to the people of Clonmel it affectionately remained 'the Mechanics'.

Despite its difficulties, it had the distinction of being the only mechanics institute in Ireland, outside of Dublin, to keep its doors continually open. It provided courses of stimulating lectures and gave the town a well-stocked library and a flourishing art school. Most importantly, the building and its facilities were to provide the nucleus of the future development of technical education in the town.

In 1899 the Clonmel Corporation took over the Mechanics Institute. It was renamed the Central Technical Institute and a committee was set up to establish a scheme of technical education for the town. The library was retained, day classes were reorganised and the night classes expanded.

The Vocational Act 1930 saw further changes in the administrative structure. The corporation was no longer responsible for the provision of technical education. That function was then vested in the VEC. The building, however, remained the property of Clonmel Corporation and this fact enabled them, with the help and encouragement of Mr J. V. Nolan (town clerk), to hand the building over to the Society of St Vincent de Paul in Clonmel when the new technical school was completed in the late 1960s.

The building housed a night shelter for homeless men for a number of years and was also used by a number of organisations over the past few decades as a meeting venue for some of the town's Conferences. It still fulfils this role and acts as a storage space for furniture, clothing, books, etc.

The History of the Society of St Vincent de Paul in Mullingar

Seamus Mimnagh

Mullingar is the county town of Westmeath and the cathedral town of the Diocese of Meath. Earliest records available start at the Annual Meeting of the Conference of the Immaculate Conception held on 28 July 1926 in the Conference room of St Mary's Hall (Parish Hall), Mullingar. The minutes of this meeting indicate the Conference of the Immaculate Conception was first established in Mullingar in 1916. We hold no records of the personnel or the activities of the Conference between 1916 and 1926. The Conference was formed in turbulent times both at home and overseas and would, in the ensuing years, have to cope with extreme hardship among a large percentage of the population. In 1929, the Conference, in its submission for aggregation, estimated the number of poor in the parish of Mullingar at 1,000, or 20 per cent of the then population of c. 5,000 (the population today is c. 17,000).

The close ties between the Catholic Church and the Society of St Vincent de Paul have been well established and in the case of Mullingar the relationship was no different, particularly in the first half of the twentieth century. On 20 June 1928 the meeting was informed of the death of their beloved patron and bishop, his Lordship Most Rev. Laurence Gaughran. He had worked tirelessly in the interests of the Society, which resulted in many more Conferences in the diocese. The Conference president, T. F. Nooney, reported in June 1928 that he had been asked to assist in the formation of a Conference in Kilbeggan Parish.

It was the custom in the Society then to have obituary notices printed and posted to the Irish Conferences asking for prayers for the repose of the soul of the member or associate who had died. This was done in the case of Bishop Gaughran. Our files also contain a few such notices, similar to notices received from Cork in 1934. His Lordship Most Rev. Dr Mulvany presided at a general meeting in December 1929. He complimented members on their work and he announced that on his recent visitations to Co. Meath he had received promises from four different parishes that Conferences would be established before the winter was over.

Organisation

In January 1930, a letter from the Council of Ireland was received, stating that approval had been given by the Bishop for the formation of a central council with headquarters in Mullingar for the Diocese of Meath. The society was at this time organised on a diocesan basis. Quarterly meetings were held locally, often after the ordinary Conference meeting, and a general meeting was held once a year. Group meetings were held on a rotational basis in Kells, Navan, Trim, Dundalk, Drogheda, Balbriggan, Tullamore and Mullingar, attended by representatives from the Conferences across the diocese. A number of meetings were held in St Finian's College. Meetings of the central council were held regularly. Two Brothers cycled from Mullingar to a group meeting in Navan (a distance of just under thirty miles) in July 1943.

In 1926, the Conference had a boot scheme in place where lists of deserving children were received from the two primary schools, St Mary's (CBS) and Presentation Sisters. This scheme was continued right up to the 1950s. A 'poppy fund' was also available for relief of ex-servicemen. In January 1929, the Conference set about establishing penny dinners in the town and recruiting a qualified nurse to visit the sick poor in their homes.

The Council of Ireland advised the formation of a ladies' committee. A special meeting of ladies from the town was held on 12 February 1929 and a committee formed to make whatever arrangements were necessary in connection with the nurse appointment and the penny dinners. Appeals were made and generous donations of money, potatoes and vegetables were received during the periods when the Penny Dinner Scheme was in operation (the scheme closed temporarily during the summer months). The post of nurse was advertised at a salary of £12. 10s. per month. Interviews were held and a person duly appointed. This nurse left in November and a further appointment was made in December 1929. Flag days were held to coincide with the holding of the Point to Point Meetings at Ardivaghan (one of the high points of the social life of Mullingar) and other functions were arranged by the Ladies' Committee in support of the Nurses Fund and penny dinners.

Members had difficulty finding suitable premises for the penny dinners until Providence intervened. The spiritual director informed a general meeting on 27 February 1929 that suitable commodious premises had become available in the Tanyard, Convent Lane, Bishopsgate Street, at a nominal rent. The premises were made ready and rotas established. Dinners operated six days per week, excluding Sundays. In February 1930, the entire management of the clinic and nursing scheme was left in the hands of the Ladies' Committee. The Conference was very active at this time, as the returns indicate. In the quarter ended 30 June 1930, the Conference reported the number of families assisted as 128. A total of 1,254 visits were made, 9,527 penny dinners were distributed and 742 visits (child care) were made by the nurse. The premises at Convent Lane were damaged by a fire c. 1962 and the Conference reverted to holding its meetings in St Mary's Hall.

In January 1932, Brothers were asked to furnish names of married men with families and unmarried men on Conference lists with a view to finding employment at the new cathedral, work on which commenced in March 1933. The formal opening and dedication of the new cathedral took place on 3 September 1936. It was dedicated to Christ the King and was solemnly consecrated on 6 August 1939.

In April 1932, the Conference discussed the decoration of the town for the forthcoming Eucharistic Congress. Many families could rest more peacefully in Mullingar following the event, as in the following November the Conference received a letter from the Eucharistic Congress Committee offering collapsible bedsteads at three shillings each, also enamel wash basins and jugs, etc. Sixty beds were ordered. A further letter was received in February 1933 stating the Eucharistic Congress Committee had reserved 100 beds for the Conference.

On 15 December 1942, Most Rev. Dr Dalton at his own wish attended an ordinary meeting of the Conference. He expressed his pleasure at being present and hearing the excellent report which had been read. He was well aware of the work being done by the Society and when coming to Meath he was grateful to know that the Society of St Vincent de Paul was so firmly established in the diocese. In April 1946, the Conference proposed a vote of congratulations to the Bishop on his being made Archbishop of Armagh and in May 1947, the Conference proposed a vote of congratulations to Monsgr. Kyne on his appointment as Bishop of Meath.

In January 1935, a new literature committee (a sub-committee of the main Conference) was formed with the intention, it appears, of purchasing Catholic literature for distribution. It was suggested that they commence in a small way by purchasing some Catholic newspapers and making them available at the next meeting. In the meantime, the members were to find out 'the number of reading cases in each district'. Members were reminded to bring Catholic newspapers for distribution.

The Conference had a seed potato scheme in operation for a number of years where it purchased seed (mostly British Queens!) and distributed it to those with a plot of ground and the will to plant. For much of that period, the Conference, through a sub-committee, operated an allotment scheme in conjunction with Mullingar Town Commissioners.

The War Years

In July 1940, the Conference discussed the possibility of a scarcity of food supplies arising. The president reported that he had arranged with two purveyors to reserve supplies of tea, sugar and flour for the Conference. On 3 December 1940, the president arranged with purveyors to take delivery of 300 lbs of tea and three chests to hold on reserve for the Conference. In February, the president paid for tea taken into stock at 2s. 2d. per lb, the usual price being 3s. 2d. per lb. In April/May 1941, a letter from the parish council was read regarding turf cutting and, following discussions with the bog gangers, the Society provided tea, loaves, butter and milk for men working on the bogs for a period.

Emergency Kitchen

In November 1943, the Conference decided to open the dinner rooms at a date to be decided after a meeting with the Ladies' Committee. An advertisement was placed in the *Westmeath Examiner* seeking gifts of vegetables from farmers and a raffle was organised. Fundraising activities included jumble sales, flag days and drives and support from organisations like the Legion of Mary. A drill display was held in the Christian Brothers (Rev. Bro Mulholland) in January 1941, with proceeds in aid of the Society, who did stewarding at the event. The army staff held a boxing tournament in the military barracks in December 1943. For the four months January–April 1945, 14,796 dinners were provided at a cost of £369. 3s. 6d. The scheme was continued in 1946 and 1947.

An offer was received from the Council of Ireland of army blankets at 13s. and mattresses at 10s. each. It was decided to purchase 100 blankets and these were distributed from St Mary's Hall on 26 March 1946. Brothers were exhorted to attend Mass and Holy Communion and pray for the beatification of Frédéric Ozanam. Leaflets were given to the Brothers to distribute to the poor and ask their prayers and Holy Communion for the cause. It was the custom for a period to increase the value of tickets distributed by 1s. in the week preceding 21 September in honour of Frédéric

Ozanam. It was recommended that weekly Catholic newspapers be purchased by the Conference for distribution to the poor.

Sunshine Home Mornington

The Sunshine Home Mornington was officially opened on 25 July 1964. In March 1962, Father Dermody, spiritual director, discussed the prospect of establishing a Sunshine Home (based on Sunshine Home Balbriggan) and how it might be funded (Sunshine Fund) at a Conference meeting. He gave an account of interviews with Brother Cashman (Council of Ireland) and Brothers from Kells and Drogheda who were all keen on the project. Later in March, Bros. Feeney and Geraghty reported on visits to Conferences in Kells, Navan, Trim, Oldcastle and Clonmellon, where the Sunshine project had been discussed. Each Conference was asked to send a delegate to a special meeting in Mullingar to be called by the Council of Meath in April 1963 – the delegate to have the authority to approve or otherwise of the scheme. The meeting decided the Particular Council of Drogheda would be asked to develop a pilot scheme for a small number of children initially. Brother Commins explained that the parish (Mullingar) needed to raise £2,000 for the Sunshine Home. Brother Feeney outlined plans for raising funds for the home, which would include flag days, raffles, church gate collections and so on.

In June 1964, Bishop Kyne, in a letter to Mr T. B. Adams, gave his permission to the Society for the proposed holiday home. It was decided that the home should cater for old people as well as children. The bishop announced he would sponsor a diocesan appeal on one day each year for the running of the home. The Mullingar Conference was extremely busy at this time, sometimes holding two meetings on the same evening. On one of these occasions in July 1964 the acting president, Brother Sexton, 'observing the nervous tension of the Brothers after two meetings, allowed smoking after the prayers, and produced a well-known brand which was passed around to the gasping brothers'!

Boys and girls were catered for separately at Mornington, up to fifty at a time. A group of boys from Mullingar (members of the local boys' club) were in occupation at the time of the opening. Conference members travelled with the boys and stayed with them for the duration of the visit.

Frank Tuohy and Willie McNamara can recall travelling with the boys. Frank remembers being in Mornington with a group of boys from Mullingar and he got the job of refereeing an 'international soccer match' between the boys in Mornington, representing Ireland, and a group of boys from Scotland who were visiting nearby. After the match all the boys gave Frank a good-natured ducking/showering with water and sand. It's a tough job being a referee! We have no record of Frank refereeing internationally afterwards!

Willie McNamara was an active member of the group responsible for the development of the Mornington project. He remembers the following people as being some of those involved: John Gerrard and John Wallace, Drogheda; M. Mullen, Oldcastle; T. Noonan and Allan Donnelly, Navan; Terry Adams, Tullamore; and Jack Kiernan, Kells. He says that the shops in Drogheda supplied food and meat for the first month.

Ladies' Committee

The first mention of the involvement of women in the organisation locally was in 1929, as already mentioned, with their involvement in penny dinners and the Nurse

Scheme. Variously referred to as the Ladies' Committee, Ladies' Clothing Society or Women's Clothing Committee or Guild, they played a prominent role in organising fundraising events such as whist drives, charity dinners, jumble sales, raffles, fashion shows, cookery demonstrations, card drives at Columb barracks, sales incorporating an auction in St Mary's Hall, coffee mornings, golf competitions and so on. They were also involved in the procurement of clothes of all types, which they gave to the Conference and which for a time were distributed by the nuns and Brothers. The Ladies' Committee regularly sought formal assistance in writing from men from the Conference when holding fundraising events. The distribution arrangements gradually changed, and in October 1964 the minutes record: 'It is planned to establish a wardrobe and issue tickets to clients who can avail of the stocks at certain given times to be arranged.' A furniture store was also opened at this time. Clothing tickets were issued to deserving families and arrangements were made to collect clothing on nominated dates and times at St Mary's Hall. Up to then and for a period afterwards, the ladies often used their own homes, garages, etc., to store the clothing, as space was limited in St Mary's Hall due to it being used by a number of other groups.

At a meeting of 22 October 1963, the Conference was informed that the Ladies' Clothing Society were anxious to become honorary members of the Society and a number would attend the next festival meeting.

Following discussions with the Conferences and headquarters, it was decided to start a women's Conference. It was the second Conference to be formed in the country – the first was established a few weeks before – but the Mullingar Conference was, according to Helen Kane, the first women's Conference to meet with the then president of the Council of Ireland, Brother Bill Cashman (RIP). The first formal meeting of the Conference of Saint Jude was held on 14 January 1964, with the following officers elected: president, Cecily Kenny (deceased); vice-president, Carmel McNamara (deceased); treasurer, Mary Oliver; and secretary, Ann Brosnan (Kelly) (deceased).

The Conference undertook various activities, including visiting elderly women in their homes and visiting long-term patients in St Loman's Hospital on a one-to-one basis, each member visiting the same patient on the same day and time each week. Some members also visited patients in St Mary's Hospital. Members brought small gifts when visiting, such as sweets, cigarettes and fruit; various amounts of money were spent, the limit was two and sixpence approximately. The membership grew rapidly thereafter and continued to be involved in providing clothing to the needy.

In May 1962, under a direction from the Secretary of Central Council, it was decided to divide the Senior Conference of the Immaculate Conception into two Conferences. The new Conference was named 'Christ the King'. The names of the members of the new Conferences were drawn from a box and both presidents were elected by secret ballot. A third Conference was established in March 1963 with the role of visiting patients in St Loman's Hospital. This was as a result of the success of visitations, which had commenced in c. 1959 by members of the Immaculate Conception Conference prior to it being divided. There were then three Conferences in the town. The two visitation Conferences operated separately for a number of years but were reunited in the 1980s. A youth Conference was established in the late 1950s and continued into the 1970s. Since then, whilst not formally registered, the students in the local secondary schools have worked closely with the Society in particular activities.

New Premises

A new premises, Ozanam House, was acquired in 1986 and following refurbishment was officially opened and blessed by Most Rev. Dr Michael Smith, Auxiliary Bishop of Meath, accompanied by Most Rev. Dr John McCormack, Bishop of Meath, on Monday, 28 October 1987, the feast of St Vincent de Paul. Later in the evening, Bishop Smith celebrated Mass with members in the parish community centre. The occasion was a joyous one; the acquisition and refurbishment of the new premises marked the fulfilment of a long-cherished dream going back many years. This was in many ways the beginning of a new phase in the work of the Society locally, as it allowed for the establishment of a thrift shop, furniture stores and meeting rooms. There was now a centre where the public could call, buy goods and/or discuss their problems.

Conferences were already established in the adjoining parishes of Kinnegad, Delvin, Ballynacargy and Turin. A Conference was established in Killucan (St Benedict's) in 2010, where it currently operates a thrift shop. The premises in Mullingar was extended in 1990. A shop Conference (St Margaret's) was established in Mullingar following the opening of the new premises in 1986 and the Society has had the benefit of a FÁS Community Employment Project over the years. The society became involved in a social housing project c. 2000 and a special Conference, St Joseph's, was established to manage the facility and other housing projects. Today the Society in the area consists of ten Conferences (five in the town and five in neighbouring parishes). Members are active in various areas of activity, including family and hospital visitation, operating thrift shops, providing holidays for individuals and families, social housing and housing-related matters.

For the past number of years the area council has been involved in providing financial assistance in the education area, helping those who would otherwise have difficulty accessing third-level education. In the year 2011–12, the Conference assisted eighty students. Great joy was experienced recently by the community and the Society, particularly those visiting patients in St Loman's and St Mary's hospitals, as the long-awaited state-of-the-art facility Cluain Lir was opened and a number of patients transferred there. The construction of the building for the remaining patients on the grounds of St Loman's Hospital is well under way.

New apartment block for Mullingar

In 2002 of a block of eight single apartments by St Joseph's Conference, Mullingar was completed. The building is located on a compact site facing the Royal Canal close to the Dublin Bridge and is within easy reach of all amenities. In letting the apartments, the Conference, without setting out to do so, achieved the perfect gender balance – the tenants are four women and four men. An excellent community spirit prevails within the group – they are all very happy in their new surroundings and take pride in looking after their apartments. St Joseph's apartments, as they are known, were blessed by Bishop Michael Smith and officially opened on 19 June 2002 by the late Mr Noel Clear, outgoing national president.

Celebration of Service

Saturday, 9 November 2002 was a very special day in the life of the Society in the Midlands. The Mullingar Area Council held a Celebration of Service, including the presentation of medals to members of the Society in the Mullingar area in recognition of their dedicated service to the Society, some with service stretching back to the 1960s and before. The celebration was held in St Paul's Church and more than eighty members of the Society attended. Mass was celebrated by Most Rev. Michael Smith, Bishop of Meath, assisted by Rev. Fr. Henry Adam. Guests included the national president, Brian O'Reilly, who was paying his first visit, as was John Hickey, the new regional president, and past regional presidents Mary O'Donnell and Theresa Pettit (deceased). The bishop gave an inspiring homily and paid tribute to the recipients and to the work of the Society. This was followed by an address from Mr Brian O'Reilly, who congratulated the recipients, who he said had given such sterling service to the Society in the name of the poor. Bishop Smith blessed the medals, which were then presented by himself and the national president to thirty-three of the forty-eight members (not all those honoured were able to attend).

Following Mass, an oak sapling was planted by the national president in the grounds of the church. This sapling was grown from an acorn taken from an ancient oak, reputed to be up to 800 years old, which stands on the site of the birthplace of St Vincent de Paul near Dax in the South of France. The acorn was collected in the course of an unforgettable pilgrimage to France in September 2000. The gloom of the November weather quickly lifted when all present retired for the evening for a most enjoyable get-together in the very pleasant surrounds of the Mullingar Arts Centre. Many old acquaintanceships were renewed with much reminiscing and discussion.

Ormond Region – St Albert, Cashel

Francis B. Egan

*T*he earliest record we have of the Society of St Vincent de Paul in Cashel is an extract from the minutes of the corporation meeting held in the City Hall, December 1869, which reads as follows: 'That the house in Agar's Lane lately in the occupation of the Society of St Vincent de Paul be let to the Parish Priest for Educational Purposes at one shilling rent per year.'

The society was in fact established in 1867 and first appears in the official lists of the Council of Ireland in 1868. The Conference was aggregated by the Council General on 20 February 1871, and so must have worked to the satisfaction of the Council of Ireland for some time. At the time of its establishment, the Conference of St Albert, Clonmel, was the only Conference in the Archdiocese. From 1867 until 1870, the Society held its meetings in the Mechanics Institute, Agar's Lane, on Tuesday evenings at 6 p.m.

In its first year, 1868, the Conference reported receipts of £42. 0s. 7d., expenditure of £8. 14s. 6d. and relief in kind of £17. 19s. 0d. It had twelve active members, an average attendance of nine at meetings and fifty-three honorary members.

In 1874, John Mullins Esq., JP became president. The meetings were held in the city hall and there is a minute of the corporation meeting in January 1870 giving permission to the Society to hold its meetings there. The Conference was then meeting on Sundays at 7 p.m. with an active membership of ten, average attendance of eight and sixty honorary members. John Mullins held the presidency for a number of years.

In December 1875, Archdeacon Quirke reorganised the existing Society of St Vincent de Paul at a meeting of the parishioners of Cashel, held in the sacristy of the Catholic Church on Sunday, 12 December 1875. Patrick Hackett and Denis O'Kearney Crux were two leading citizens of those days. Patrick Hackett lived in the Green (the house is still to be seen) and was a brother to James Hackett, father of the family of that name that is still living in the Clonmel Road. He was also brother to Father John Hackett, who, after being curate in Borrisoleigh, acted as chaplain for the Christian Brothers in Cashel for some years. The Hackett family were the ancient patrons of the Franciscan Church in Cashel, which stood where the present parish church now stands. The holy water font still used in the parish church was the original stone coffin of a Hackett chieftain.

The Cashel branch of the O'Kearney family were the hereditary custodians of St Patrick's Crozier and were known by the honoured title of O'Kearney Crux.

As may be surmised, the resources of the Conference were very limited during its earlier years. The main source of income deserves comment. A number of boxes were placed on the counters of bars and shops throughout the town. Very often they were filled weekly. For example, we find that on 8 April 1876 the following sums were acknowledged by the Conference as received from the boxes:

Dolan & Co.	£1. 3s. 7d.
Mrs Dunne	6s. 0d.
Mr Mullins	4s. 9d.
Mr Peter Connolly	5s. 6d.
Miss Ann Dwyer	11s. 10d.
Mr Hayden	5s. 6d.
Mrs P. Hackett	3s. 11d.
Miss Quirke	1s. 7d.
Miss Anne Hanly	1s. 3d.

This total of £3. 5s. 0d. (almost) is a handsome sum for one week. The names quoted are those of honoured Cashel Catholic families who were the leading citizens of Cashel throughout the seventies and eighties of the nineteenth century.

The work of the Conference during the early part of the 1900s shows little variety. The records from 1914 to the present show that the Conference meetings were held every week with a good attendance of members and the spiritual director rarely, if ever, absent. When one considers that in half a century 2,500 meetings were held, we cannot but admire the persevering charity of the members. Relief was in the form of tickets, which had to be taken to a particular purveyor. One could not fail to notice the increase in the value and number of these tickets during World War I. At Christmas, the number of tickets increased remarkably and many homes got both fuel and food. In February 1917, the number of applicants was 124 because of a very heavy snow storm. The ticket has since completely disappeared and help is given in the form of a money grant.

A welcome addition to the usual work of the Conference came in 1926, when there was entertainment given in the then county home by the Brothers. There were songs, music and a band recital. This work continued and the following year they purchased fruit and other ingredients to get barn bracks made for the inmates. A letter of appreciation was received from the county council.

It was during the 1940s that the Conference work really expanded. Visitation became regular and the needs of families were attended to. At that time it was customary at the meeting of presidents to read extracts from Conference reports. In 1947, the following excerpt was read from the Report of Cashel Conference:

'The work which gave us most satisfaction was the distribution of bedding and blankets purchased through the scheme initiated by the Council of Ireland. We purchased £40 worth. On investigating the most deserving families we found the sleeping conditions appalling. It was only after persuasion the parents consented to us seeing for ourselves.

'We found a family of eight with two beds and practically no covering. To them the bedding and blankets brought comfort and joy. Within a week an empty bedroom had been washed clean and beds neatly arranged for the children. At our next visit the proud mother insisted on our seeing the transformation.

'To a family of ten who were sufficiently grown up to be segregated, beds and bedding were most welcome. Separate beds were immediately erected by grateful parents.

'A third family of eight had just welcomed one of its members home from a TB hospital. It was imperative she should not sleep with the others. With a mattress and blankets from our Conference, a separate comfortable bed was easily put in order and a mother's anxiety allayed.'

Since the 1940s, the work of the Conference has embraced all forms of charity. These include:

- Seaside holiday each year for 160 children.
- Seaside holiday for deserving adults.

- Old folks' party at Christmas.
- Entertainment at St Patrick's Hospital.
- Installation of electric light.
- Cleaning and decoration of homes.
- Supplying dinners at Christmas.
- Regular visitation of St Patrick's Hospital.
- Blanket Scheme.
- Wardrobe Scheme.

Gradually, different forms of charity were required, which included meals on wheels, education, food, fuel, etc. In early 2000, the region received a generous donation, and at the bequest of the donor, the money was set out for education. The main outlay at present is education grants to third-level students and a small number of mature students. There are also a small number of grants for childcare, to enable mothers to improve their situation. Fuel, oil, electricity and other utilities all have increased in demand. Attempts are made to meet all clients, have the necessary forms completed and make decisions at weekly meetings.

Meals on wheels is still going on as an independent unit, using the house kitchen, and run as part of social services. Social services have their own staff now. FÁS also have the use of an office in the house.

As a result of the centenary, there is hope for a big extension of the Society in the town, and the SVP looks optimistically to the future.

Tinahely – The Making of a Conference

Eileen Flanagan

*E*arly in 2011, a call went out from the Society in south-west Wicklow for people interested in setting up a Conference to come to a meeting in our local community hall. What this would involve no one knew, and those who attended came along for a variety of reasons. My own were simple enough. As a journalist, I had reason to admire and respect the work of the Society throughout my career. My only personal involvement had been to donate on national collection days but it was through my professional life that I had drawn on the expertise of the Society when it came to assessing and writing about the impact of government budgetary changes on the less well-off in our society.

Spokespeople for the SVP, like Professor John Monahan, through their public statements on behalf of the Society, were people you could rely on to obtain factual information on conditions for those living on minimum wages and families existing below the poverty line with no prospect of changing their lives.

Tinahely is not untypical of many rural areas. It is situated in south-west Wicklow, just north of the Wexford border.

A particularly scenic area, it attracts many hill walkers each year. It is mainly an agricultural community, but some light industry and business developments have been established over the years. Whilst there is local employment, the majority of people have to commute to work. Rural transport links are minimal and the nearest towns are some fifteen miles away. During the early 1990s, six private housing developments were built in and around the village and homes were mostly acquired by people working in Dublin or by people who had retired. The population of the village and surrounding area has expanded tenfold during the past decade.

At the very first meeting, David O'Neil, administrator for the south-east region, and Edmund Roche, area president, introduced us to the work of the Society. By the end of the meeting, most of us were hooked. What was set out before us at that and at subsequent sessions was a presentation of a modern organisation where not only were functions and roles clearly defined, but comprehensive training was put in place to enable ordinary people like ourselves to act in a way that would support and help people to cope with difficult periods in their lives. Over the next ten weeks, various aspects of the work of the Society were covered, culminating with a visit from regional trainer, Monica Hillery, who instilled a sense of confidence in us all when it came to dealing with visitation.

At our final training night, we met Regional President Kieran Stafford and it was then that we formally made the commitment to set up our local Conference. We did so in the knowledge that the region would be there for us if we ran into any difficulty dealing with problems that were beyond the scope of either our ability or expertise to address.

Within a few weeks of setting up the Conference, a unique opportunity came our way when the manager of Wicklow Farm Relief Services, Joe O'Brien, offered us a large shop in the village centre on a trial basis for eight weeks to see if we could create a focus for the Conference in the area and this was an opportunity to become financially self-sufficient. The idea of setting up a shop had already been suggested by some of the Conference members, but funding it would have been too big a drain on our resources and it was felt what money we had needed to be available to help people in need. To be offered a shop, free of rent, for eight weeks to see if it had the long-term potential to generate income for the Conference was a wonderful opportunity and the Conference decided to run with it.

Two weeks later, on 17 May 2011, we opened for business. Volunteers were enlisted to work in the shop and they remain at the heart of the success of the project, as without them we could not have achieved what we have over the past twelve months.

David O'Neill provided us with ongoing support and advice, as did Kitty Hynes, head of the South-East Regional Shops Committee, Maureen Murphy, president of the Bunclody Conference and Bridget Braham of the Gorey Conference, all of whom run highly successful shops. Without their help I doubt if we would have succeeded. Sharing with us their insights and experience was invaluable and made the difference between success and failure.

Eight weeks later, the shop was well established and we had negotiated a sustainable rent with our new landlords. Support for the project came from everywhere: from within the Society, from the local community and from villages and communities within a fifteen-mile radius of Tinahely itself. We were inundated with donations. Parallel to this, we continued to learn on the job, with volunteers and Conference members attending a shop training night in Gorey organised by David O'Neill, Kitty Hynes and Bridget Braham. And we haven't stopped learning. We know that at any time, if there is something we can't deal with, we can pick up the phone and there is someone there to help and advise us. The value of this type of backup and support can never be underestimated.

Whilst visitation remains at the heart of the work the Conference does, we have identified a range of needs in the community that are compounded by its isolated location and the harsh downturn in the economy. Following the SVP Older People's Commission, we have researched the needs of the elderly in the area and find that they are the group facing the greatest difficulties. We hope to focus in the coming months and years on developing services to meet their needs.

Would we do it all over again? I think for all of us the answer would be 'Yes'. Little did we know how events would unfold when we started out last year, but the opening words of that famous song, sung by Edith Piaf, '*Je ne regrette rien*' is a fair summary of how we feel now. The work is rewarding, challenging and it is great to be part of a modern, compassionate community organisation that strives to embody Christian values in a practical way on an everyday basis. Our thanks to David, Edmund, Kieran and Kitty for showing us the way.

The History of St Vincent de Paul in the Mid-West Region

The mid-west region of the Society of St Vincent de Paul has responsibility for activities in Limerick, Clare, North Tipperary and south-west Offaly. This history of St Vincent de Paul in the mid-west region is based on a combination of surviving records and previous publications. Brief histories of the Society have been compiled in the past, such as *Glimpses of the Society of St Vincent de Paul in Limerick*, which was published by the Society. More recently, however, a very informative publication by Bob Ryan entitled *An Open Door – The History of the St Vincent de Paul in Limerick 1846-1996*, has been an invaluable source of information for much of the content contained within this chapter.

However, all who have been engaged in this type of research have faced a common problem: a lack of individual stories from members, whose memories and experiences have the ability to bring to life the history of the Society in a manner dusty old records could never do. As Ryan correctly highlights, the Society has always tended to conduct its work quietly and efficiently, with a greater emphasis placed on responding to the needs of the time rather than record keeping. Therefore, although there are a certain number of records to consult, such as minute books of meetings, correspondences, old journals and so forth, many are missing the human story, which is very much part of the history of St Vincent de Paul.

Therefore, the use of oral history by way of interview, where memories of members are digitally recorded and archived, can supplement the Society's record books and reveal the more human, and often times more light-hearted, side of the Society's work. It also has the added advantage of preserving the experiences of older members in order to inform young members.

Ultimately, what can be said about the Society of St Vincent de Paul in the mid-west region is that the history of the Society itself is set against the backdrop of historical events, which, although quite challenging and often hampering its work to a certain extent, brought out the best in its members. In essence, from a historian's perspective, the Society can be viewed as a social barometer, being an indicator of stressful times.

Pre-establishment

Many people will be aware that the name St Vincent de Paul was only adopted as an archetypical name for what the founder of the Society, Frédéric Ozanam, wanted the it to reflect; it was felt that de Paul was a good example for the Society to use as a role model due to his endeavours in helping the poor. However, not many people will know that the mid-west region had in fact a tangible link to the saint long before the introduction of the Society to Ireland. This link exists due to the then Bishop of Limerick, and friend of Vincent de Paul, Edmund O'Dwyer, who in 1646 wrote to him with an invitation to send members of his congregation on a mission to Ireland. As a result, a contingent arrived in the autumn of that year. So impressed was he with the success of this mission, Bishop O'Dwyer wrote to de Paul stating that, 'I can assure you that their labours have produced more fruit and that they have converted more souls than the rest of the clergy together.' Thus, 200 years before the establishment of the Society in Ireland, Vincent de Paul's influence was being felt in the mid-west region.

Establishment

Nevertheless, leaving this direct connection between de Paul and the mid-west region to one side, the Society that exists today was founded in Paris in 1833 and in little over a decade it had spread to Ireland. Its introduction to the mid-west region can be described as a baptism of fire, given the difficulties it faced and the demands put upon it. The establishment of the first Conference, that of St Michael's, in November of 1846 coincided with one of the most difficult periods in Irish history: the Great Famine.

And so the Society had taken its first step in what would prove to be a long and arduous journey with the poor of this region. And poor they were, for it had been the opinion of some notable visitors to the region, such as Ingles, Thackeray, and Kohl, that 'they were more wretched men among the poor of Limerick than in any town of equal population in Ireland...'

The famine had exacerbated the pitiful conditions of the poor. Indeed, an increase in the number of people seeking refuge in the workhouse worsened in 1847, with massive migration from rural areas to the towns. This, coupled with poor sanitation and a lack of medical services, led to the spread of cholera, typhus, dysentery and other diseases, all of which made the work of the Society a daunting task. A welcome development, however, was the formation of an additional Conference, that of St John's, which was established on 20 February 1847. In fact, such was the work of its members that it was reported that the Conference of St John's parish within a short period distributed an 'amount of relief ... in a manner and efficiency ... that no poor law could ever hope either to reach or rival'. Thus, despite the difficulties encountered by the Society during its initial introduction to the mid-west region, it was nevertheless able to have a positive effect in such difficult circumstances. These early Conferences were later joined in 1856 by the Conference of St Mary and St Munchin. There were also Conferences during this period in Rathkeale, Askeaton, Ballingarry, Kilfinane, Glin and Bruff and later still in 1889 when St Joseph's became the fourth Limerick Conference, all of which toiled for the betterment of the poor in the region.

There were of course other upheavals during the nineteenth century which the Society had to contend with. Foremost of these was the greatest social problem that affected Ireland in the nineteenth century: the land question. Evictions had been continuing for many years, the worst being between 1849 and 1853, a period often referred to as the 'land clearance'. Although the Society endured a difficult beginning in the mid-west region, it nonetheless equipped its members for what was to follow in the next century.

The early twentieth century brought some of the greatest challenges to the Society, such as both world wars and the revolutionary struggles in Ireland. However, it was also a period of much improvement, which saw the establishment of the Nursing Association, the youth Conferences, and also moves to establish a headquarters for the Society in Limerick.

Conditions for the poor of the mid-west region, particularly Limerick, had certainly not improved at the

57

turn of the century. Given that many still lived in deplorable conditions in houses that were very badly ventilated and without basic sanitation, it was no wonder that the effects of these conditions resulted in sickness among the poorer class being rampant. To cater for the growing number of sick, the Ladies' Society of St Vincent de Paul, originally founded in 1897, engaged the services of a maternity nurse, Mrs Williams, to attend to the poor in their own homes. Such work was performed against the backdrop of military hostilities both at home and abroad.

Although Ireland was not directly involved in World War I, it was nevertheless affected by the shortages caused by the conflict. The worst of these shortages was food. It was envisaged that a scheme known as Workman's Gardens would have the ability of addressing this shortage. Under this initiative, working-class families were to be given allotments of land by the local authorities and encouraged to produce their own vegetables. The society's primary concern with regard to this scheme was ensuring that families that had been visited by the Conferences would not be overlooked in the allocation of plots, as in some places land was limited. The end of World War I in 1918 should have perhaps ushered in a new period of stability. However, although hostilities in Europe had ceased, rising tensions in Ireland led to new challenges for the mid-west region and its people.

In 1920 the country was still in the grip of the War of Independence and the curfew imposed by the Black and Tans on the people of Limerick affected the attendance at meetings. Furthermore, while visitations by members continued, they did so at great personal risk to themselves. Yet despite the difficulties of the War of Independence, the Conferences continued with their work. In particular the Youth Conference was very active, with works including the circulation of Catholic Truth Society literature amongst college students, holding raffles and social entertainment. Following the War of Independence and the ensuing Treaty, the country had to endure a civil war which, while quite brief, greatly infringed on the work of the Society. For instance, curfew regulations interfered with the progress of the plans of the Society to establish a boys' club, and the idea of a secretariat for the poor had to be abandoned. Furthermore, although a committee was formed to distribute relief tickets to the poor during this period, which when presented at the food depot entitled each person to certain provisions, collecting such provisions could be dangerous given that on several occasions the food depot came under fire, and on at least one occasion the distribution had to be abandoned. Other infringements at the time included the cancellation of the July quarterly meeting.

Ozanam House

In 1917, it was felt that in order to carry out the Society's work effectively, it should have a home of its own in Limerick where the poor could readily have access to advice and assistance. Thus, negotiations commenced to purchase Hartstone House from the Order of Hibernians, whose City Division were the trustees of the building. In the 1880s it had been the home of the O'Maras, who owned the Limerick Bacon Factory. Stephen O'Mara, who for many years had a close involvement with the SVP, was an Irish nationalist MP in Westminster and later a senator in the Irish Free State while also serving as mayor of Limerick. On one occasion, his brother, a well-known opera singer, entertained the people of Limerick by singing from the balcony of Hartstone House. Therefore, this particular property was already well known in the city.

And so, on Sunday, 22 February 1920, Ozanam House was officially opened by the Bishop of Limerick, Dr Hallinan. The bishop stated that he believed that its opening would mark a new epoch in the history of the Society in Limerick and would be the beginning of a new era of multiple activities.

Some of the first special works to be carried out at Ozanam House included the provision of a boys' club, a library, and a secretariat for the poor, where they could come for advice. Lectures, debates and discussions pertaining to the activities of the Society were also held. All of these works supplemented the main work of the Society, the visitation of the poor in their homes. Ozanam House still acts as the headquarters for the mid-west region.

Boys' Club

As mentioned above, one of the first special works carried out at Ozanam House was the establishment of a boys' club. This was undertaken by the Society in the late 1930s with the opening of St Brigid's Boys' Club for the underprivileged boys of St Mary's parish. The original clubhouse, which was located on the Island Bank of the city, was offered to the Society by the parish priest of St Mary's. However, the man who was largely responsible for the founding of the club was Ned Tracey, a solicitor who devoted his life to the boys of the club.

With the outbreak of World War II at the close of the 1930s, the Society was once again affected by external forces. Many of the original members of the boys' club joined the British forces and fought in the war. Some of them never returned home. The war itself, like other armed conflicts, brought pressures on the Society as imported commodities such as coal, petrol and oil soon became quite scarce. To address this situation, members of St Brigid's Boys' Club spent the summer holidays of 1941 working in the bog at Castleconnell helping to cut turf, which Muintir na Tire distributed by operating a turf scheme from Ozanam House. As a result, it could be said that many of the boys made sacrifices in the name of the Society of St Vincent de Paul during this period and enhanced the reputation of the boys' club, which boded well for the future. Alas, on 15 April 1961, St Brigid's Boys' Club on the Island Bank, which had been vandalised and broken into on many occasions, was destroyed by fire. However, within a year a new premise was found in the Castle Barracks from which to continue the boys' good works.

Banks

Established in 1919, the Conference of SS Mary and Munchin operated a penny savings bank on Friday evenings at Gerald Griffin Street School. The idea behind the bank was to encourage saving among the poor. They proved very successful in encouraging thrift.

In later years, especially during the hard times of the 1980s, one of the more serious problems the Society encountered was moneylending, which was deemed a menace to people living in the large housing estates in the city. Many families, as well as borrowing from moneylenders, would get into arrears with bills such as rent or ESB.

Thus, during the 1980s the Society concentrated on getting to the root causes of poverty by running educational courses in the region. These courses dealt with budgeting and money management. Talks were given on how to budget income, and demonstrations were given on how to cook cheap meals. Members also advised people on a one-to-one basis in their own homes. The initiative was so successful that the Mid-Western Health Board adopted the idea and ran a similar scheme called Family Support Workers.

1930s

The 1930s are remembered as the time of the Great Depression, where the Wall Street crash resulted in an economic slump and increasing unemployment. This of course led to greater demands on the Society. It also saw many changes. One of the greatest and most far reaching was the rehousing and relocation of many Limerick people. This in turn led to many difficulties, as these new houses were much larger than the people's previous ones and the shortage of furniture and bedding was aggravated by the fact that the little furniture that they had, which consisted mainly of boxes used as tables and chairs, was grossly inadequate. Other non-material issues were also of concern, such as people missing their old neighbours and feeling isolated and extremely lonely. Furthermore, it was difficult to pay the rents as they had increased from one shilling to four or five. Again, secretariats were formed to advise the poor of their rights and entitlements.

The 1930s also saw the formation of new Conferences in Kilfinan and Kilmallock.

Work with Travellers

The society, as many members will be aware, has always strived to help and improve the conditions of marginalised people. One such group were those of the Traveller community. This was achieved by firstly setting up St Martin's Conference to deal specifically with their problems, and secondly by gathering as much information on the topic as was possible. Questionnaires were sent to all Conferences throughout Ireland in 1978 in order to find out what contact and services were being provided and to get the views of Conferences about the main problems facing Travellers. Among the findings to emerge from this process was the belief that the Society should embark on a long-term plan for at least a period of one generation in order to establish a personal relationship with Traveller families, rather than occasional help, which was deemed useless. Furthermore, it was suggested that efforts should be made to persuade the government and local authorities to provide halting sites as well as priority being given to educating the public about the needs and problems of Travellers.

Therefore, a working party was set up to examine the problems of Travellers in the mid-west region and to make recommendations on their needs. This grouping made several recommendations designed to solve some of the more pressing problems, such as the provision of standpipes for clean water, the provision of sanitary facilities by way of a Portaloo, a skip to hold domestic refuse and arrangements for regular removal of this refuse. Provision of an animal enclosure and a permanent halting site with all these facilities was also recommended.

However, the main difficulty with the plan was where to locate the halting site. This problem dragged on for ten years until eventually the Travellers decided to take the matter to the High Court, which ruled in their favour. As a result, the Corporation built many of the halting sites that exist today in the mid-west region. The action of the Limerick Travellers in particular, and the building of the well-equipped halting sites by the Corporation, set an example for the rest of the country. Furthermore, St Martin's Conference set up workshops for Travellers, training them in various crafts and educating them, a fact which was recognised by President Mary Robinson when she visited Ozanam House in 1995.

Penny Dinners/Hostel, The 1950s and 1960s

Following the end of the war, the Society in Limerick celebrated its centenary in 1946. This was also the year that they introduced Sunday breakfasts, or 'penny dinners' as they were often called. These were primarily for the elderly and homeless and could be had at 10 a.m. each Sunday in Wembley Hall in the Watergate area of the city. Here the men were given grilled sausages and puddings and as much bread and butter as they could eat.

A special committee was appointed by the Council of Limerick to consider the possibility of providing a hostel for homeless men. The matter had been considered before but the acquisition of suitable premises had been a stumbling block up to that point. Since the 1950s there had been a growing awareness by members of the need for a hostel in Limerick for older homeless men.

At the beginning of the 1960s it was agreed to purchase the former residence of the highly respected Canon Frederick Langbridge, which was once a nursing home where a number of Limerick's prominent citizens were born: Number 3 St John's Square. This was one of the old town houses in the square and was of great architectural value to the city as these were amongst the oldest inhabited buildings in the city. Indeed, the doorway of Number 3 was the finest of the ten houses in the square. Thus, St Patrick's Hostel was formed.

Prison Committee

During the 1950s the Society took an active role in helping to solve the problem of juvenile delinquency when some members acted as probation officers. A Juvenile Care Committee was set up and the Conference, which was aggregated in 1952, was named after St John Bosco.

However, this was not the first foray into such matters, as in 1904 prisoners' aid work was undertaken by the Society, which aimed at finding employment for prisoners when they were released from prison.

Twinning, the 1980s

In 1986, Sierra Leone on the west coast of Africa was twinned with the mid-west region. To formalise the twinning, the president of the Society in Sierra Leone, John Turay, travelled to the region dressed in full ceremonial African clothes, which was his way of honouring the occasion.

Housing the Homeless in Recent Years: Hostels, Social Housing, Drop-in Centres

In recent years, the SVP has been very responsive to the problem of homelessness in the mid-west, in particular in the area of hostels and social housing. St Patrick's Hostel in Limerick caters for forty-five men; the volunteers and staff work with each individual to develop an individual care plan. This method is also employed in our newly opened thirteen-bedroom hostel, Laurel Lodge, located in Ennis, Co. Clare.

Our hostels provide an invaluable service to individuals experiencing severe personal challenges. Some past residents have come to live in the SVP hostels as a result of family or marital breakdown; for others SVP hostels have provided a home after release from prison or following the completion of a drug or alcohol treatment programme.

Nationally, the SVP is the second-largest provider of social housing after the government. In the mid-west region, we operate twenty-three social housing units in Limerick city; these units are available to those aged fifty-five and over. The SVP also opened a twelve-unit social housing project as part of Ennis Town Council's Westbourne Housing Scheme. In many cases residents of SVP hostels find a more permanent home in an SVP social housing project. Other residents have come to us as a result of domestic abuse, family difficulties, or as a result of having a specific housing need.

The sheltered nature of the SVP social housing projects means that individuals who might not otherwise be suited to independent living have the opportunity to have a home of their own.

One of the SVP's most successful homeless services is the SVP Drop-in Centre, located at the regional office on Hartstonge Street. The centre provides refreshments as well as shower and laundry facilities to those who are homeless or at risk of becoming homeless. The interventive nature of this service means that individuals who are at risk of becoming homeless are identified early. Our Drop-in Centre manager, with the assistance of a dedicated team of volunteers, works hard to ensure that such individuals receive the support necessary to prevent them from becoming homeless. Such supports can include referral to a drug or alcohol treatment programme, help to find suitable accommodation, support to access employment, training or a second chance at education; an average of fifty-five individuals access this service on a daily basis.

Section Two

The Society of St Vincent de Paul Remembers

Expressing, Experiencing and Exploring Connections

*Kieran Murphy, National Director of
Saint Vincent de Paul*

T he SVP is an extraordinary organisation, and one for
which I have worked for ten years. Since starting in
2003, I have at times been challenged, inspired, frustrated,
grateful, angry, always busy and never bored! As I look
back on those ten years, I can see that there have been
a few key moments of insight which have helped me to
understand the organisation and thereby sustain and refresh
my commitment to it. Often these moments of insight
are the answer to a question or questions which have been
gnawing away at me over an extended period of time. The
most interesting questions for me have been not about what
we do, but why we do it. Questions such as: does Ireland
need the SVP now more than ever? What is the purpose of
the SVP?

The SVP is extraordinary because of the range and
variety of its work: active in each of the thirty-two counties,
almost 10,000 volunteer members, around 500 employees,
providing a wide variety of services and all done by a
membership-led organisation. It has often occurred to me

that if the SVP did not exist, and I spoke to a management consultant looking for advice as to how to set up and run an organisation of the scale and complexity of the SVP, they would design a very elaborate organisation with lots of levels of management and specialists to train, support and supervise the work. Yet what we have is almost the exact opposite: almost 10,000 volunteers within 1,000 Conferences all over Ireland, busy getting on with their own work, week in week out, without anyone checking what they are doing. This does not always work well for Conferences, and it often presents challenges, but this local autonomy to get up, get out and get on with the work is an extraordinary quality of the SVP.

Coming to work for the SVP was a difficult transition. The scale and complexity of the organisation took me a while to get my head around. I was used to working with single-issue organisations where there was one focus, such as lone parents or housing, etc., whereas the SVP is involved in a wide variety of activities.

One of the first challenges I encountered was to try and understand home visitation. I remember a car journey from Sligo to Galway, late 2004, with someone who was familiar with home visitation and discussing at length with them what exactly its purpose was. There was something about it that I just did not understand. I could see that there was a need for people to be given material and emotional support and that there was a strong demand from the public for visits. However, home visitation was a very different kind of service than anything I had encountered before and I really struggled to make sense of it. Here were volunteers visiting people in their own homes rather than having people visit the organisation's offices; volunteers who provided financial support and yet were not financial advisors, who listened to people's problems and yet were not trained counsellors, who provided advice and guidance and yet were not social workers. There were lots of elements to the work but I was missing a piece of the jigsaw needed to make sense of it. I could see, at a surface level, that it was in demand, but I just could not figure it out. It did not correspond to any of the usual service models with which I was familiar.

The more I looked at home visitation and listened to the volunteers doing the work, the more I began to understand its unique nature. I could see that the volunteers were moved by the needs of people in their own community and wanted to respond. Most people are moved by the plight of others, but one of the qualities of Vincentians is that they want to do something about it. But there was more to it than that. I could see that the volunteers were having some of their own needs met as well: they wanted to help others and this helped them feel better about themselves and about life and its value and purpose. There is nothing wrong with this. What it illustrates is that there is a reciprocal relationship between the helper and the helped. And in some respects the helper is also the helped, in that their need to help others and to be satisfied through their helping is being met.

What I began to see was that the volunteers were expressing their sense of being connected to other people by being moved to respond to their needs. They were also experiencing a sense of connection through the relationships they had with other members of the SVP and with the people they visited. Furthermore, there were signs that some were exploring the nature of this connectedness through engaging with some of the challenging questions posed by the work, e.g. why is it that some peoples' life circumstances are so different to their own, in terms of the challenges they face and the problems that they encounter?

Expressing, experiencing and exploring connections between people is the way I describe the underlying purpose

71

of home visitation. I'm not suggesting that every volunteer, when they call at a door, thinks that they are expressing, experiencing and exploring human connectedness, but when I peel back the various layers of meaning underneath the work of home visitation this is what I see. This has been an important answer for me and it links home visitation to a much broader vocation of what it means to be human. It is what the Jewish faith calls *tikkun olam* — humanity's shared responsibility to repair, heal and transform the world.

One of the questions that sometimes arises, particularly in relation to our special works, is 'Why is the SVP doing this work?' At one time I would have been of the view that it is the government's responsibility to provide a service for people who are homeless. Therefore, the reason the SVP is one of the largest providers of services for people who are homeless is because of government failure: if the government was doing its job, the SVP would not need to be involved.

Like many things in life, the answer to the question about why we are involved is neither black nor white. Over the years I have met several of the volunteers involved in setting up and running our hostels. Our newest service is in Ennis, Co. Clare. When I first began working for the SVP I had contact with the Conference and they were determined to provide a service in Ennis. Their commitment, energy and relentless pursuit of their vision impressed me. They could see from their daily journeys in and around Ennis that there was a need for a service for people who were homeless. For many years, they held onto their vision. They talked to people within the SVP, talked to their local authority, the Health Board, local politicians and commissioned a piece of research to evidence the nature and extent of the need within Ennis. Without their vision and commitment, there would not be a service in Ennis today.

What this illustrated for me is that communities have a role and a responsibility to respond to the needs of people within their community who are homeless, and that if we hand over this role exclusively to the government we will never succeed in providing sufficient services. That is not to say that I'm letting the government off the hook; I'm not. They have an important role to play, specifically in relation to funding. But a service devoid of community involvement will not be effective.

This point was brought home to me when I met a manager of a homeless service not run by the SVP. In response to my question, 'How are things going?' he explained that their service was great at providing emergency accommodation, helping people deal with their addictions and other problems they have, sourcing move-on accommodation and supporting them to move into accommodation beyond the hostel. But, he went on to say, we can't solve homelessness.

We are all sustained in life through the quality of the relationships we have with other people. When a homeless person moves into new accommodation, they often find it intolerably lonely and they miss the companionship of the street or the hostel. So homelessness is not simply solved by putting a roof over someone's head, but by helping them to re-establish the network of relationships that will sustain them. My colleague commented that this was beyond the capability of his service, but it was something that the SVP could do through its volunteer network. My view now is that it is the government's role to fund the services, and it is the communities' role to advocate for a service in their area and to provide the human supports necessary to help people live independent lives beyond the street and the hostel.

When I consider all the work of the SVP carried out by members, volunteers and employees, I wonder about the motivations that prompt this work. At the heart of the work of the Society is an impulse, from our members, volunteers and employees, to respond to the needs of other people because they are moved by their life stories and circumstances. This is a deeply human instinct and a form of love. The ancient Greeks called it *agape*. Like all forms of love, is it reciprocal: both parties experience a giving and receiving, but create something that is greater than the sum of the two parts. Are all our members, volunteers and staff motivated by pure *agape*? Of course not! We all bring a complex mixture of motivations and needs that shift and change over time, but at the heart of it all is an instinct to engage with and respond to the needs and circumstances of another human being.

A reservation I had when applying for the job was the religious nature of the SVP: the way in which prayers and Masses are a feature of meetings, and that the Catholic origins and ethos are explicitly important for the SVP. In my own faith journey I had arrived at a place where traditional Catholic prayer and spirituality practices no longer held much meaning or provided nourishment. I was nervous that there would be a requirement in the job to be 'religious' and that it would be uncomfortable for me. I need not have worried. I quickly realised that among the membership and employees there are all faiths and none, and that while there are many who are inspired and nourished by the prayers and Mass, there are equally many who through their work are expressing some deeply held values. These groups happily coexist with neither being asked to adopt the creed of the other. My own faith journey has continued through the last ten years and my involvement with the people and the work has shown me that there is something extraordinary about the instinct in people to reach out to and help another human being. Judy Cannato, the American spirituality writer captures it beautifully when she writes, 'The significance and magnificence at the heart of even the most ordinary aspects of life.'

President Higgins greets SVP National President Geoff
Meagher at Áras an Uachtaráin when the Society undertook to
support the ethics initiative launched by President Higgins.

Mairead Bushnell – the first woman to become SVP National
President in Ireland and Vice-President John Monaghan
launch the SVP Pre-Budget submission to Government in
2010. Social justice campaigning is a focus of SVP work.

Being a member of the SVP can be fun.

Serving those in need with heart and mind is an integral part
of Society work and young members are essential for the future
of the organisation.

International SVP President Michael Thio chats with a resident in the SVP Hostel in Waterford. SVP hostels are part of the Society's work to help the homeless.

SVP fundraiser at Cork City Hall.

The annual Teenage Celebration is a big SVP event for schools in Waterford.

Opening a new SVP shop at Kiltimagh in Co. Mayo.

SVP Drogheda funraising fun run, one of many public events
run to raise finance for the work of the Society.

The Vincent's bridal store in Terenure, Dublin.

President Michael D. Higgins addressing the SVP national commemoration to mark the Ozanam Bicentenary at the National Convention Centre in Dublin in 2013. Frederic Ozanam who founded the SVP was born in 1813.

Art project designed by members of SVP teenage
integration project.

Frederic Ozanam, who founded the SVP in Paris.

So, what does the future hold for the SVP? There will always be a need for organisations like us, which provide services and financial supports. But we can't afford to be complacent, because things change.

There is a large granite trough in Smithfield in Dublin and engraved on the side of it are the words 'Metropolitan drinking fountain and cattle trough Association'. It dates back to a time in the mid 1800s in London when there was no clean running water in cities and it posed significant public health hazards and meant there was no reliable source of water for cattle in city markets. This trough is a reminder to me that organisations come and go in response to the needs of the communities in which they operate. 'To go' is not a sign of failure and 'to stay' is not a sign of success.

If the SVP is to thrive over the next twenty years, its future must not simply be seen in terms of providing a quality service to people in need. We must do that, but we must do more: we need to reimagine our core work, home visitation, by making explicit and integrating into the purpose the needs of and benefits to the volunteers who carry out the work. That would mean a shifting from a service *to* people to a service *between* people. To do this would reenergise the work to the benefit of both the visitor and the visited.

Fifty Years A Vincentian: A Personal Journey

Liam Fitzpatrick, Treasurer General Saint Vincent de Paul

*I*joined the SVP early in 1962, a job transfer having brought me to Cork a few months beforehand. I will readily admit that it wasn't Vincentian idealism that motivated me. Indeed, it was a work colleague who suggested that it was a handy way of spending a cheap night out each week and, with money being scarce, it seemed a pleasant prospect. I knew nothing about St Vincent de Paul at that stage. However, in the fifty-one years that have elapsed since then, that knowledge deficit has been much reduced, not just about the Society, but also about life generally and especially about a sector of society whose lifestyle and attendant issues are far different from those faced by the more comfortable.

In the course of my membership, I have been fortunate to experience many facets of SVP work, such as home visitation, mental hospital visitation, children's holiday home, job creation, men's hostel and clothes collection and distribution, which was the forerunner to Vincentian shops in which I also served. My membership has also been enhanced by the fact that I have had roles at different levels, including Conference, area and regional presidency, national board and national sub-committee membership. In particular, I regard it as a privilege to have been asked to serve as international treasurer, a post I currently hold.

I do not write this to give the impression of an important contribution on my part, but to convey the range of activities open to members, especially in urban areas. SVP membership has been a very important part of my life and I am firmly convinced that it has had an extremely positive influence on me as an individual. I certainly believe that I have got, and continue to receive, much more from my Vincentianism than I have put into it.

I hope it may be of interest to give a brief summary of some of my early Vincentian work. My first experience was in a home visitation Conference which, like all Conferences at that time, was made up entirely of male members. It may be hard to believe now, but women were not allowed to join the Society until around the mid-1960s. Our visitation area was in a relatively new Corporation housing estate of forty to fifty houses in the north side of Cork City, where the majority of the residents were either permanently out of work or were casual dockers. We called to most of the houses in the estate with food vouchers, supplemented by the occasional voucher for fuel, clothes and shoes (redeemable at city shops). I can still recall the sense of real poverty which we met – very little furniture in the kitchen, a mother and kids huddled around a very poor fire, a diet consisting in many cases of little more than tea and fried bread and the anxiety of the mother that she and her family might be dropped from our visitation list. In most instances, it was the mother who carried the burden, very often with little or no support from the father.

Simultaneously, we visited male patients in a large local mental hospital. Mainly we called to men who were long-term residents and whose condition was relatively mild. Very often they had been abandoned by their families and faced the prospect of spending the rest of their lives there. They were happy to see a face from outside the institution, but it took some time to gain their trust. Having created a bond with them, however, it was obvious that they looked forward to our weekly visits. Bearing in mind that TV was relatively new then, many of them had little knowledge of or interest in what was going on in the outside world, and the conversations with them tended to be repetitive and very narrowly focussed. Looking back on it now, it is sad to think of so many who were committed to and left in mental institutions when they could have been cared for outside.

In addition to the visitation Conference, I also joined a special works Conference which operated a summer holiday house for young boys and girls at the seaside some fifteen miles from Cork city. As holiday homes go, it could hardly have been more basic. It could best be described as a roofed shed with windows – no electricity, no running water and dry toilets. The children, aged from about eight to twelve, loved it. Some of them would never have seen the sea previously and the idea of a week's holiday at the seaside was paradise to them. We employed a cook and had the services of young volunteers, mainly clerical students, who gave up a week or more of their summer holidays. By the standards of today, there was little emphasis on health and safety or hygiene and, while we did our best within the confines of what we had, it would be unthinkable now to run an operation along those lines. Thankfully, and only by the grace of God, we had no serious accidents or other problems.

Towards the end of the 1960s, we commenced a used clothes operation which involved the collection of clothes from donors, sorting them and distributing them to callers to the Cork office or through Conferences. I still have memories of driving into residential parks, in response to telephone calls from donors offering clothes, and trying to locate houses armed only with the surname and the name of the house. Having eventually found the right house, the frustration could well be exacerbated when you arrived back with your load to find that it was mostly rubbish! The businesslike way in which the shops now operate is a far cry from that initial venture.

Since those bygone days, Ireland has changed immeasurably and the SVP has also changed enormously. We are in such a completely different world that I don't think it is relevant to make direct comparisons. Some observations may, however, be valid, but they come with a health warning as they are entirely subjective, based on my personal experiences.

In the Ireland of today, the SVP is needed more than ever. Fifty years ago, the Society provided material aid to those in need through home visitation, homeless hostels, etc. Now, however, the need is for much more than material aid. Many of the people we visit in their homes or who live in our hostels have other complications in their lives, including broken relationships, addiction problems and counselling/psychiatric needs. These call for different skills on the part of our members, who need to be able to recognise the symptoms and know the extent to which they can help and, more importantly, when to stand back and refer the situation to professionals.

Also, fifty years ago, the SVP was not as involved in advocacy as it is now. In the current climate, being a voice for the poor is a very important part of our activities. Without a well-informed and professional input on their behalf, there is a grave danger that the interests of the less well-off will be neglected, and the SVP has sufficient standing that its views carry weight. Our exhortations do not always yield the desired results but, without our voice, it can safely be assumed that the assistance provided to the poor by the national government would be considerably less than it is.

The question is raised occasionally as to whether the work the SVP does should be done by government or public bodies. In a perfect world, the answer is probably yes. However, visiting people in their homes builds up a relationship which could never be matched by the public service. The bond which is created between our members and those we visit is something that can be unique to both parties and becomes much more than just a call and a voucher. Similarly, in our hostels, each resident is linked with a case worker and a programme is drawn up to meet the particular needs of the individual resident. Obviously, these programmes don't all work perfectly but at least they provide a platform from which progress can be made. Another aspect of our hostels which cannot be disregarded is cost – in St Vincent's Hostel, Cork, which houses seventy-five men and of which I am a Conference member, the cost to the public purse of providing full board, accommodation and care works out at about €12,800 per person p.a. (2012 figures). This is only a fraction of what it would cost in a public institution.

On a national basis, one can only imagine what the cost would be if the many hours of voluntary work put in by our members in different areas had to be done by public servants.

In my time in the Society, the most rewarding results for me were probably from two particular works:

1. Seeing the enjoyment on the faces of children in our holiday house in Ringabella in the 1960s. Despite what were fairly spartan conditions, it was magic to

them to experience a holiday at the seaside and the nightly parties.

2. Seeing the benefits of our education grants. People who would never have had the opportunity to attend university have graduated with the help of the SVP and, in many cases, were the first members of their families to acquire a degree.

On the reverse side, the most disappointing aspect has been the fact that the SVP continuously finds itself helping successive generations of the same families.

Are we sometimes helping to perpetuate poverty? How do we overcome this? Education is undoubtedly a vital element.

The make-up of SVP in Ireland has changed radically over the years. When I joined, there were very few employees and we boasted that all our administration expenses were met by our members through the secret bag collections taken up at meetings. How the situation has changed since then! Nationally, we now have some 600 employees plus 120 employed under CE schemes and, while the Society is still volunteer-led, we could not function in today's world without professional support. It is just not possible for volunteers in Conferences all over the country to deal with current requirements under such headings as finance, health and safety, child and vulnerable adult protection, charity legislation, etc.

A large proportion of our membership see their involvement as confined to their particular Conference and, with so many other demands on their time, this is perfectly understandable. It is necessary, however, that a sufficient number take on roles outside the Conference. Otherwise, the various councils and different functions that arise at all levels of the Society could not be catered for. While appreciating that each member has different circumstances, it would be good for the organisation overall if there was more member interaction outside the confines of his or her own Conference. Also, many retired members have skills that could be of great benefit in the Society's administration.

The most rewarding role for me in my SVP membership has been my appointment as international treasurer general in 2010. Prior to that, like so many other members, my knowledge of the Society worldwide was sparse and, when asked by the current president general to take on the role, I was apprehensive, asking myself, 'Why am I taking this on at this hour of my life!'

I have to say now that it has been a most enlightening and humbling experience for me and has broadened my perspective very considerably. It has enabled me to meet society members throughout the world and I have acquired some sense of the poverty which exists in third-world countries and more so of the difficulties under which our members in these countries have to operate. The SVP has 45,000 Conferences in almost 150 countries, but only a small perecentage of these countries could be termed first-world. The depth of poverty in many of the others is appalling and, if I was given a wish, it would be that first-world countries like Ireland would become more involved in helping our Vincentian brethren in these countries, mainly in Africa and Asia.

I fully appreciate that there is poverty in this country, but it is at a different level to that experienced in many others. I also realise that members in Ireland give support through twinning and through the SVP's international aid system. The need, however, is huge and sharing some of our resources could make a significant difference in relieving very severe conditions in different places abroad. If we are isolationist in this regard, we are not being faithful to the spirit of our founder, Frédéric Ozanam.

Am I glad that I accepted the invitation to join the SVP in 1962? Absolutely, yes! My Vincentian experience has given me many friends, has provided me with a life balance that I wouldn't otherwise have had and, without wishing to sound smug, has enabled me to give something back in return for the many blessings which it has been my good fortune to enjoy in life.

Dedicated Vincentian Mary Toole Served with Distinction

Bill Lawlor

O ne of Ireland's most dedicated and longest-serving Vincentians, Mary Toole of Navan, whose deeply regretted death occurred in January 2013, had seen huge changes in Irish society in general and the effects upon it of poverty, particularly in recent years.

As someone who, since 1973, filled top SVP posts at Conference, regional and national levels, her sympathetic and knowledgeable approach to problem solving proved an invaluable asset to the organisation she so willingly served.

Over the decades she had a frontline view of the circumstances that have shaped the problems that today confront the Society of St Vincent de Paul and indeed the community it works for.

She was convinced that the type of poverty encountered by volunteers today is much different and more difficult to deal with than the more obvious hardship of previous times.

In an interview some months before her death, she said: 'In those days you knew that by buying a family a bag of coal you were probably doing much to solve their problem.

The situation today is much more complex as debt-laden families and individuals try to cope with ongoing dilemmas, including near record levels of unemployment.

'We must also recognise that poverty is relative and not by any means straightforward, because there is now a fine line between need and want.'

As an example, she cited how everyday 'luxury' items are regarded as essential for normal living.

'Years ago, someone in need of help would almost certainly not have even a black and white television in their home. Now, a state-of-the-art plasma TV prominently displayed in the living room of those seeking assistance is usually just regarded as part of the furniture and certainly doesn't mean that they are not worthy of aid.'

Mary, who was a retired employee of An Teagasc in Navan, was the first female member of the Society in the Meath town, having started her SVP career with the local St Oliver's Conference, of which she was a member and former president.

She also served, at various periods, as Navan Area President, and president and secretary of the North-East Regional Council.

However, it is probably through her impressive contribution to the Society's role in overseas assistance via the twinning programme that she was better known throughout the country. She resigned some time ago as national twinning officer, but continued her work as regional council up to the time of her death.

Referring to the demands on current members, she believed there was a definite need for training of Conference presidents. 'The most important person in the Society is the Conference president. He or she has the important responsibility of encouraging members and helping to deal with the problems they encounter,' she stressed.

Looking at the Society today, she noted that a spiritual dimension to their work is not always as prominent among members as it was in their counterparts of previous times, and she wondered if there was a sufficiently strong motivation to observe Christ's gospel proclamation: 'Whatever you did for one of the least of my brothers and sisters, you did it for me.' (Matthew 25: 31–46).

A colleague, Catherine O'Connor, of Navan SVP's St Oliver's Conference, in a well-deserved tribute, stated that despite her achievements at Conference, regional and national level, 'Mary maintained the true Vincentian spirit in her everyday work with the Society, which is an example to all members, both old and new.

'Her help at Conference meetings in solving problems about which we were unsure was invaluable and her suggestions were always appropriate. When it came to questions about the Rule of the Society, she was also ready to clarify.

'Mary was very keen on finding new young members and encouraging them to take up officer roles within the Conference and later the area and region. It is because of her humility and trust in others that we have such vibrant Conferences in Navan.

'Her skills as area secretary and input to the operations of the Vincent's shop in Navan were invaluable. Indeed, without her help we would not have a shop. It was she who initially suggested appointing a manager. She dealt with FÁS with regard to shop assistants, looked after all the accounts and was there to help whenever there was a problem. Indeed, the shop committee would agree, she always managed to solve these difficulties.'

Catherine pointed out that, since her retirement, Mary devoted all her spare time to the Society and the members were extremely appreciative of all her work behind the scenes.

Catherine added: 'Because of Mary's efforts we are a vibrant organisation in this area and very active in visitation and helping the poor and needy. With regard to visitation, she was an excellent listener, asking all the right questions in an unobtrusive manner – always making excellent suggestions without ever being condescending.'

The Late Dan Fox: Generous, Dedicated – and Unsinkable

Bill Lawlor

D an Fox was booked to travel on the ill-fated *Titanic* maiden voyage. But in 1912, as he was about to depart for the US, his mother, who had been knitting his socks, insisted she hadn't enough time to finish the task. So she persuaded him to change his ticket and leave at a later date. He subsequently did go to America. However, he returned after some time to become a dedicated Vincentian.

In the 1930s and 1940s, Dan was a member of St Eunan's Conference, Letterkenny, the oldest in Donegal. It was founded in 1879 and named after the patron of the parish. His daughter, Kathleen, herself a member, recalls that in the early part of the twentieth century the Conference met on Sunday mornings after Mass. She remembers her father would then go home, have his dinner and set out on his visitation. As a young child she accompanied him on these treks, 'walking huge distances to the outskirts of the town.' Fascinated, she watched as he delivered slips of different-coloured paper to the homes they visited. Years later she discovered that these were for a food store, a shoe shop and a clothing shop – the forerunner of the voucher system.

Kathleen and her dad would return for their tea and then set out again for another part of the town. Out in all kinds of weather, Dan was regularly exposed to the worst of the elements in the picturesque but sometimes harsh conditions of Donegal. So his wife saved up and bought him a really good overcoat. However, not long afterwards, he returned home without the coat. He felt someone's need was greater than his.

Dan, who died in 1947 aged fifty-three, was just one of the members at that time who, without the benefit of transport or phones, operated with generosity and dedication. Among the others were Henry Allison, Pop Coyle, Dr McGinley, Mr Mahony and Brian Walsh.

'All of them were true Vincentians,' says Kathleen.

Where It All Began

Rose McGowan, Dublin Regional President

The seeds of my membership of the Society of St Vincent de Paul were planted many years ago when, as a young student in the Dominican College, Eccles Street, we were encouraged to become involved both in sporting activities and in doing some activity that would benefit those less well-off than us. Our school was situated not far from Dublin's inner city, so we were accustomed to seeing poverty first hand, but also to 'pass by' and not think about it, until we were encouraged by the Dominican Sisters to 'unite in head and heart in some charitable work' (to quote from Blessed Frédéric Ozanam). All my motives for becoming involved in the Society were not of the highest level at all times – we were conscious of the boys from Belvedere College and Colaiste Mhuire, joining with them to raise funds by way of carol singing, which was exciting and great fun and for some of us had lasting benefits!

So my journey of love began at a very early age. The practical work of the intermediate mixed Conference was hugely enjoyable and fulfilling. We spent our free time carrying out basic tasks, such as painting the flats of the many elderly people we visited, wallpapering, sitting, chatting, and fundraising. There was a great sense of fun and friendship and most of these friendships have lasted to this day. We were also greatly nurtured in our work by the 'senior' members of the local Conference, who took us under their wings, guiding us, sharing their wisdom with us, and most of all enriching our lives with the story of Blessed Frédéric and St Vincent de Paul. These men were the true followers of Monsieur Bailly, who encouraged Ozanam and his companions when they formed the first Conference.

I learnt quickly – became totally immersed – and after a few years joined the senior Conference, of which I am still a member. Frédéric Ozanam often spoke about the importance of forming an association of mutual encouragement for young Christians where they could find friendship, support and example. And this we did in our Conference – we were all starting out on life together, sharing friendships, romances, starting families, saying farewell to loved ones.

The society has been a thread running right through my life. My husband, Hugh, was a member of the Conference who went carol singing and remains a member of the Society – my children have lived with me reminding them, particularly at Christmas time, of the importance of giving to those who have little, and they are both very aware of their responsibilities to look out for others. Both help greatly when we go to Kerdiffstown Holiday Centre each year to look after 100 guests, having been first introduced to this great work while still in their prams!

Over the years I have held various roles within the Society, including Conference president, area council president, and Dublin regional president. During my term as Dublin regional president, meeting members, witnessing their dedication to our work and their openness and willingness to embrace new initiatives greatly helped me in my role. Being of service to people was the theme of my presidency. The words of Sister Rosalie Rendu to Frédéric

Ozanam before he made his very first visit to a poor family continually ring in my ear: 'Be kind and love.'

However, my first love is and will always be my weekly Conference meeting and visitation.

You may be familiar with the quote of Blessed Frédéric: 'Charity must never look backwards, but always to the front, because the number of good deeds already accomplished is very small, while present and future hardships remain infinite.' This challenge was very much in my mind when, as area president, I was asked to look at the development of Ozanam House, Mountjoy Square. This fine property had been let run down for many years, and was used primarily for Conference meetings and the awfully named 'Salvage Bureau'. Conferences issued dockets to people they visited, for clothing, shoes and bedding, and these were presented at the 'Salvage Bureau' and the docket holders were given the goods. At the time I was asked to undertake this project, I was conscious from my visitation work that what was needed was a resource centre, somewhere for elderly people to come to during the day, a crèche to enable mothers to return to work and education, a place for young people to meet other than hanging around street corners. A small group of members from Dublin North Central Area Council got together and were lucky to attract funding from a number of sources and proudly opened Ozanam Resource Centre ten years ago. Today it is a hive of activity with something for everyone in the audience! This project has been one of the joys of my life and I am indebted to all the Conferences who continue to support it.

As Dublin regional president, I promoted the mission of the Society – support and friendship – working for social justice – promoting self-sufficiency. I feel strongly about support and friendship – really getting to know the people we visit, sharing our stories with them, remembering birthdays, encouraging talents and enabling them fulfill their dreams.

I have now been privileged to be asked to take responsibility for the national twinning programme and have been appointed by the President General Michael Thio to the Commission for International Aid and Development.

During my presidency I was delighted to visit Zambia, which is twinned with the Dublin region. Witnessing the poverty first hand, but also seeing the difference a small amount of money can make to the lives of the people the Society in Zambia visit has given me new energy to make our twinning programme a success. The friendships we formed during our visits continue today.

My life and that of my family has been greatly enriched by my membership of this great organisation and I constantly remember with great affection and thanks the Dominican Sisters who encouraged us to undertake works of charity; the members of that intermediate Conference – now our husbands and friends – and in particular the men of the senior Conference who, by their example and encouragement, imbedded in our hearts a love of helping those less well-off.

It has been and remains a wonderful blessed journey for which I give thanks daily.

> *There is need to feel remembered, by others, to tell ourselves*
> *that we are not alone. There is need of support, of comfort,*
> *of prayers ... Friendship is precious.*
>
> (Letter to M. Gorse, 1836)

Playing a Pivotal Role in the Community

Mary Sheridan, North-West Regional President

In 1990, I was invited to join the Society of St Vincent de Paul, an invitation I reluctantly accepted simply because it was an organisation that appeared to work quietly in our midst with no publicity and their good deeds virtually unknown. For me it was a move into the unknown, with no training, no induction and no mentor – you virtually learned by example. How times have changed.

At that time, it was predominantly an all-male Conference, but I was in awe at how sensitive they were to people's needs and the sincerity shown both in the work and to the spiritual ethos of the Society, for they firmly believed you could not have one without the other. We should always remember that the spiritual element of our society is the one thing that makes us different from any other charity or organisation.

With visitation being the core work of the Society, I was afforded the opportunity to live out our mission statement by providing support, a listening ear, and by befriending people in their own homes. I learned to treat people with dignity and respect. The important thing to remember is that when we entered people's homes it was a privilege and we were guests in their castles. All too often our visits are rushed but what I know is that when you treat people the way you would like to be treated, then you can't go far wrong.

The principle work of our Conference at that particular time was visitation to the elderly and families, with a huge emphasis on improving living accommodation where necessary. But the problems that existed in our communities then still exist now: isolation, loneliness, budgeting and debt.

One of my most memorable visits was to a lady who lived on her own in a remote area on her birthday. We brought her a birthday card, flowers and chocolates. It was as if we had given her a million euro: the smiles, the tears, and the thank you we received. She was so appreciative because it was her first birthday card ever and she was in her eighties. She had made our day too, and made us realize the difference we can make to people. It's the thought that counts rather than the amount we give at times.

Communities change and this has resulted in people not knowing their neighbours. Families have gone to explore opportunities in other parts of the world. Generally, the family unit would not be as strong today as it was in the past. Families would have sat down to have at least one meal together, where they could sit and talk, communicate and support each other. This no longer happens; TV dinners are the norm and everyone is doing their own thing. The importance of our visitation is much more relevant now, as we can sit and talk or, more often, simply provide a listening ear.

Our Conference was very fortunate to receive a large bequest, which empowered us to become real activists, and enabled us to provide a social activity centre for all sections of the community. While the bequest covered approximately one-third of the cost, it encouraged our members to work tirelessly to fundraise and source the balance required to provide the facility.

We worked closely with the Society both at area and regional levels, with statutory bodies – our local county council and the HSE – to provide a facility that could be used by all and has since become the heart of the community. Our centre is open two days per week, with an average attendance of thirty-five to forty people per day. We provide them with meals, social activities – art, computers, armchair exercises, music, dance, bingo, card playing and above all meeting up with their friends, old and new. We also provide laundry, chiropody and hairdressing services.

While this has been a huge achievement for our community, we are indebted to the HSE for their ongoing support in providing funding for the operational side of this service.

The challenge for our society and the community is to extend the services we deliver while at the same time improving and maintaining the building itself to the highest standard possible. For our Conference, the vision of providing such a facility for years and now having achieved that goal has certainly made a difference. Things only happen if you make them happen, and while this does entail a lot of hard work, it gives us, the members, a great sense of fulfillment. One of the most important things that has happened is that the people who use the centre have made it their home away from home and that is how they value it.

The society can play a pivotal role in communities but we should be careful not to live in the good name of the SVP, but rather judge ourselves on the contribution we make.

In rural areas, one of the most difficult problems for people in need is seeking help in the first place, as the members are often known to them. This is still a major problem throughout the Society – finding and helping those who have been forgotten – and we need to make it easier for people to contact us. I find so much rests on the work we do and how we do it. It is essential that people's needs are met to the best of our ability and, by promoting self-sufficiency, we can really make a difference in people's lives.

I have found that through networking with other organisations and by continuing to highlight inadequacies when we meet them, the rights of people in need are not ignored. People become very isolated, anxious and live in fear when they have a lack of knowledge, and they need us to highlight their cause. The society has been lobbying the government on our behalf and this is something that needs to continue to happen. Only our members can ensure this continues, as they have the knowledge of what is happening on the ground. If the Society's voluntary contribution was to be withdrawn, it would create a huge headache for the government.

Our world is not a very fair place to live, but everyone is entitled to the same opportunities, so we can only attempt to bridge the gaps.

The SVP Conference should be at the heart of every community and also the centre of everything that happens within the Society. That is, if we are to follow in our founder, Frédéric Ozanam's, footsteps. We need to ensure that what is happening on the ground is communicated through all levels of the SVP, so new ideas and our experiences are made known. Our work is carried out in a confidential manner and this must be maintained for the people we serve and for the integrity of our society and, importantly, in order to retain the confidence of the public and our donors. Unfortunately there are Conferences that continue to work in isolation. They are unwilling to endorse new ideas and new ways of working but they should always remember that to live is to change and we should never be afraid of change provided we are part of it.

There are a number of characteristics which are key to the success of any charitable organization and they are as follows: transparency, accountability and clear communication flowing throughout its structure.

It is above all the giving of oneself to another and in doing so we are giving our most precious gift, that of *time*. For our communities this is so very important. I know for sure that if I had waited till I had time on my hands then I probably would never have joined the SVP.

Confidentiality, simplicity, integrity and courage are all traits which have been very evident in the members that I have been privileged to work with over the past twenty-three years. In my opinion, the Society affords the opportunity to quietly but effectively make a contribution to improve your community. It also assists in the development of people through good works and, let me emphasise, without the need to embark on an ego trip, something which it totally alien to our organisation. There is one thing for certain: we will never change the world, but we can change people's lives for the better if we are prepared to go the extra mile.

From Being Helped to Member to Regional President

Aidan Crawford, Northern Ireland Regional President

Never did I contemplate becoming a member of the SVP, although I did know of the Society while growing up in rural Northern Ireland as they had helped my family.

I was the second eldest of a family of eleven and poverty was a reality for us. We survived on hand-me-downs; wearing each other's clothes; our firewood would come from us going around the fields cutting branches off trees, and in a good winter we somehow got peats for the fire. We had no electricity in the house and we used a Tilley lamp for light. My mother worked miracles in keeping us clean and feeding us, as father was unable to work due to ill health.

We were not treated very well by some of our neighbours or indeed by some of our relatives! We were the poor relations.

I remember the men from the Society of the SVP bringing us bags of potatoes, sometimes carrying them on their shoulders, other times on the crossbars of their bicycles. This was a God-send and they helped us in other ways as well.

I left school at fifteen and got a job. Later in life I married Patricia and through hard work progressed to owning my own engineering supplies business. I was then living in Ballymena, Co. Antrim.

Then it happened!

One day, my next-door neighbour, who was a sergeant in the RUC – the Royal Ulster Constabulary – approached me and asked if I would join the local Conference of the Society of St Vincent de Paul. He explained the workings of the SVP Conference, the local branch, but it took quite a bit of time before I finally joined that local Conference, not knowing exactly what to expect.

It was what I would consider the 'old hands' who were really committed to the Society at that time. In the early days of my membership, I sat there for nearly a year without doing any visitation to families – the basic, core work of the Society of St Vincent de Paul. It was necessary to earn the respect of the 'elders' before doing this visitation work. During this time I was involved in picking up and delivering furniture. The work being done was fantastic and the number of people looking for assistance kept increasing. One of my memories was of the old hand who would go out on a visit and ask a person they were helping, 'Were you at Mass on Sunday?' If the answer was in the negative, the request for help may not have been looked at favourably, but that was then and things have changed a lot and much for the better, with the training of members for many years and the insistence on respect for those we are helping through the Society. Nowadays, such a question would not be acceptable to the Society or any of its members.

Help is given to anyone who seeks it because suffering and deprivation are not decided by religious beliefs.

My development in the Society really took off when I went to the SVP Centre at Kerdiffstown House in County Kildare for training, a system developed and insisted upon by former National President Brian O'Reilly, also a man from the North of Ireland, and Cecelia Curran. The SVP is a thirty-two county all-Ireland society and justifiably proud of its work and commitment in this regard. The benefit of this training system led to my becoming Conference president. This was a large and very busy Conference, with a big amount of cases and requests for assistance to deal with.

New ways of helping those in need were introduced, including the development of the SVP charity shops, all helping to provide the funds needed with support from the parish and public, which was fantastic – and still is.

Many times during my term as Conference president we dealt with heart-breaking cases – homelessness, child poverty, suicides and more examples of the human difficulties and suffering which people, deprived of opportunity and hope or simply fallen on bad times, often suffered from.

There were also, on the brighter side, successes in the voluntary work of the Society. One case I remember particularly well is that of a young couple who arrived at the parochial house with a suitcase!

They had come from Estonia and had been promised a home and a job by an agent they had paid but, unfortunately, they had been conned and it was Christmas Eve when we got the call. No home for them on this particularly evocative day. We met the couple and discovered the young lady was pregnant. Her husband broke down and cried, pleading with us to get somewhere for his wife to stay. Amazed by what they had heard on this day of all days, with many members under the pressure of looking after their own families for the festive season, our Conference still mobilised and swung into action. Within a few hours we had got them into a furnished house with heat and food.

This story stands out for me as it reminds me of another young couple years and years ago who also were in the same predicament with no room at the inn, a story which is the centre of the Christmas celebration. The young couple now have a family of four and have been living and working in the town ever since.

After having served as Conference president, a year later I was elected area president. This was quite a different role – having responsibility for and liaising with eleven SVP Conferences in the area, with monthly meetings and working together to bring in new projects. I was fortunate that all eleven Conferences had members highly committed to the cause of helping the needy. There were, of course, inevitably problems to be dealt with, which were overcome and I learned a lot from working with individuals and groups.

In my final year as area president I was asked to put my name forward for the post of regional president. I considered it, not really knowing the ins and outs of this task, but the outgoing regional president, Cormac Wilson, mentored me and when I took up the office I was well informed. However, even though I had a good knowledge of things, I quickly discovered that being regional president is a daunting task, effectively being responsible for leading the Society, which is volunteer led but also has professional staff employed. With all their support, in a region where the Troubles have left unfortunate legacies in communities, we have still given help where and when needed and have worked across the religious divide to bring that help.

Now, as a member of the National Management Council of the Society and a trustee, I am very much aware that decisions have to be made for the good of all and that the future of the Society of St Vincent de Paul in Ireland and the help it gives to the less fortunate depends on the many dedicated members and supporters helping us in our work of relieving poverty.

On a personal journey, I have come a long way from receiving help to being in a position to give help, thanks to the Society of Saint Vincent de Paul.

A Privilege

Michael Murphy, Mid-West Regional President

*I*n 1983, a meeting was called in my local parish to seek volunteers to form a Conference of the Society of St Vincent de Paul.

I had recently returned to the parish to live and work and had been involved in a number of organizations in the area at committee/management level. I have always believed that people should be proactive in their local community and use their skills and spare time for the benefit of the whole community.

I became a founding member of Our Lady Help of Christians Conference, Ennis Road, Limerick and am pleased to note that since those initial days the Conference has continued to grow and flourish. My knowledge of the work of the Society at that stage would have been similar to most people, in that I knew it provided help to people in distress, but I was not aware of the depth of services provided throughout the city and county.

My parish is a typical middle-class parish where, at that time, there was little call or requirement for assistance. Our Conference decided to work in a neighbouring parish that had a high level of local authority housing.

The conditions pertaining to the houses we visited were certainly a far cry from those to which most of our members would have been accustomed. Today, everybody is conscious of the recent downturn in the Irish economy and the huge levels of unemployment and emigration. In the 1980s, the bleak employment situation, high inflation and rampant emigration brought back memories of the dreadful poverty of the post-World War II era, which lasted until 1960.

Successive governments from the 1960s onwards spent large sums on providing local authority housing to replace the Dickensian slums in which many families had to raise their children in the first half of the twentieth century. Unfortunately, while acceptable housing had been provided, little thought was given to providing other services within these communities. This area was a typical example where over 600 houses were built with no adequate shopping facilities in the immediate area and a very limited bus service to the city centre.

I have always felt that a major impediment to the development of a strong, vibrant community spirit in many local authority housing schemes was the £5,000 local authority grant provided in the early 1980s to any householder who surrendered their council house and moved out of the area to build or purchase their own home. As a result, many local authority tenants, who were in full-time employment, availed of this grant and consequently the level of unemployed families in the area soared to levels of upwards of 70 per cent.

This was the situation in which my own Conference found itself in our early days. I found families struggling to survive on their welfare payments with no safety net to meet unexpected expenses. At times I marvelled at how harassed mothers coped with the multiple demands on their meagre finances. I was highly frustrated with the attitude and lack of support from State bodies, whose only interest appeared to be in cutting costs and saving funds.

There was little innovative thinking in government/local authority and I quickly became involved in the social justice aspect of our work. Typical examples of the narrow thinking and inflexible system was a situation wherein the city council had a large number of rent collectors visiting houses weekly to collect rent, while at the same time the Department of Social Welfare was paying out significant amounts of unemployment benefit weekly. Many a time rent collectors would contact me regarding large rent arrears that had accumulated resulting in eviction notices, and tenants would seek our assistance in helping to meet these debts. Thankfully, due in no small way to the lobbying of the SVP, most local authority tenants now have their weekly rent deducted at source, ensuring that the threat of eviction is no longer a constant worry.

Another frustrating situation was the difficulty in arranging split payments for families. Irresponsible fathers were in a position to squander the weekly social welfare funds and leave their wives and children to depend on charity to survive.

In the past twenty years I have seen a new group of young, more understanding social workers and community welfare officers take over and our society has developed an excellent working relationship with these officials which has been mutually beneficial.

As time moved on, I became involved in the administration of the Society both in the mid-west region and nationally. I passionately believe that it is not enough to deal with the effects of poverty, but we must as a society attempt to influence the government in order to tackle the root causes of poverty.

On a personal basis, I have had many good as well as bad days in my Vincentian work. At times I feel frustrated and wonder if my visit makes any difference to the person seeking assistance from the Society. In particular, I have found in many cases a great apathy among young mothers who have become dependent on a welfare culture and do not have the initiative to try and break the cycle of poverty into which they have fallen. Generational poverty is a major concern and I would contend that our education curriculum is not geared towards developing the life skills which are lacking in the households I visit regularly. Basic hygiene, budgeting, cookery and household management skills should be a part of the school curriculum at all levels.

Any tenant who is allocated a local authority house should have to undergo a course on their responsibilities in maintaining their property and their obligations in respect of the surrounding community. I sincerely believe that the failure of local authorities to deal with irresponsible tenants quickly in relation to antisocial behaviour has been a large contributing factor to the state in which so many of our housing estates find themselves today.

When I was growing up over fifty years ago, there was much poverty, but what I did notice was the determination of many poor parents to ensure that their children had the opportunity to provide a better life for themselves. Sadly, I would contend that today I perceive a feeling of hopelessness in many of those who seek our assistance.

At times I despair of the misguided priorities of some, particularly in relation to spending at Christmas, First Communions and funerals, resulting in the accumulation of significant debt. I then realize that maybe these events are the only highlights in a very humdrum, monotonous lifestyle.

Sometimes I wonder why I continue and then remind myself that I do it for the unfortunate children who find themselves in these situations through no fault of their own.

I have tried to think of some of the more rewarding situations in which I have found myself and would admit that many of these would relate to helping young people attain academic qualifications with some small assistance and encouragement which our Conference can provide. The annual Christmas hampers and toys and the relief and joy that they provide to harassed parents and grateful children are another example.

On a national level, I take great pride in the pioneering work of our local St Martin's Conference which, with the help of a young senior council member, and later president of Ireland, Mary Robinson, took a High Court action that resulted in local authorities being forced to provide halting sites for the Travelling community. This happened thirty years ago and I am delighted to see that Eugene Feely and Bill Moloney of this pioneering Conference are still active members of the SVP. This is an excellent example of seeking to root out one of the prime causes of poverty and deal with something that the Irish State ignored for the first sixty years of its existence.

Why do I remain an active committed member?

The answer is pride in what our society represents, which is the freely given gifts of time, possessions and self in the hope of helping our fellow human beings.

I am humbled by the amazing work carried out by our thousands of volunteers, quietly, without seeking any reward or recognition for themselves. A great example would be our Drop-in Centre here in Limerick, which was established over ten years ago to help provide food, clothing, washing facilities and friendship to those who are homeless or in no fixed abode. Tom Flynn, Noel Harty, and their dedicated team of volunteers provide this service to upwards of eighty people daily.

Another example is the great work of our revision classes for Junior Certificate and Leaving Certificate students, which goes on from October to March annually. Mary Trainor and her team of teachers and student teachers deserve our deepest gratitude. Without their help, I know many of the students who attend these classes would have dropped out of school. Now, as a result of their unselfish efforts, these young people have the opportunity to go on to third-level education and are probably the first members of their extended families to do so. At times it is easy to forget that many of the opportunities we are able to provide to our own children are not available to those who depend on the SVP for financial assistance.

Finally, the dedication and commitment of our staff never fails to impress. Evidence of staff commitment to the Vincentian ethos can be seen in the number of staff who are also volunteers. I do not think that it is possible to work in our offices, resource centres, shops or hostels without a genuine interest in and empathy for the work of the Society.

The personal highlight of my thirty-year involvement with the SVP was sitting down with a mother one winter's evening and listening to her read aloud an article in our local newspaper. For over forty years, this woman had been unable to read or write and this was a momentous occasion for her. As she explained to me, she had once brought home tins of dog food to her hungry children because she was unable to read the label.

My time in the Society of St Vincent de Paul has been a privilege. It has helped shape my beliefs and my attitude to my fellow human beings. It has shown me how fortunate in life I have been to have the opportunity to offer the hand of friendship and support to those who seek and need our assistance.

Section Three

The Work of the Society of St Vincent de Paul

111

Letterkenny Hostel: A Huge Asset to Donegal

St Colmcille's Hostel in Letterkenny, which owes its origin to the efforts of a group of St Vincent de Paul members, is now widely acknowledged to be a huge asset to Co. Donegal.

As in many parts of Ireland, the problem of homelessness was a cause of grave concern in the early 1990s. It was this situation that prompted the SVP volunteers to come together and form a committee. After many meetings with other organisations and a lot of groundwork, it was decided to look at supplying individual self-contained units, rather than an open-style dormitory.

The enterprising group was offered three townhouses, which they purchased in 1994 for £100,000. Pat Harvey, then CEO of the former North-Western Health Board, provided advice and assistance to the members. The hostel opened in 1997 with four family units. Ciaran Maguire was appointed as manager. He lived in the building.

It soon became obvious that more units were required to meet the growing demand upon the facility, so a second building was erected on land at the rear of the original units and opened in 2003. The landmark hostel now has six family units, two single units, three one-bedroom apartments and a unit for the disabled. Mary Maguire was appointed as an outreach worker after funding became available for the provision of such a post. Further refurbishment of the living quarters was carried out in 2012.

North-West Regional Council Vice-President Kevin Cooley, acknowledging the vision of the original committee, says they are owed a huge debt of gratitude: 'We salute them all and thank God for the commitment and dedication of all involved.'

The founding committee was comprised of: chairman, Jim Nallen; secretary, Anna Nallen; treasurer, Seamus Clerkin; and volunteers Colm McManus, Mary McCloskey, Bridie O'Shea and Sadie Dawson.

Sadly, Seamus Clerkin died in 2006 and Anna Nallen in 2009. She is widely acknowledged as the driving force behind the project and was tireless in working towards realising her dream. Jim Nallen and Sadie Dawson of the original committee are still members.

A Winter's Tale: The Story of Cavan SVP's Night Shelter

Bill Lawlor

The huddled figure lay motionless on the church steps. The man had been there all night in the freezing temperatures, and his frost-covered clothing now glistened in the early-morning sunshine.

It was this reflective misery that first struck a shocked and dismayed young nun who came across the scene on her way to Mass. She did what she could to temporarily ease the plight of that homeless wayfarer, but it was pitiful sights like that that led Sister Margaret of the Poor Clares Order and members of the Society of St Vincent de Paul in Cavan to establish a night shelter for men in the town in 1985.

They belonged to St Patrick's Conference and their haven, named after Our Lady of the Wayside, provided a much-needed facility for men in the locality sleeping rough. 'There were five of these around the town at the time,' recalls Anselm Lovett, a former president of the Society's North-East Regional Council. Most of these were in derelict cars, but SVP volunteers of that era tell tales of desperation, with one man sleeping in a phone kiosk, another in a barrel, while one particularly intrepid man made himself comfortable in a coffin after managing to get into a local undertaker's premises. Perhaps it was a life or death dilemma for that wretched knight of the road.

There was no easy solution to this persistent problem in the rural town of about 4,000, but the Conference tackled it by initially buying seven derelict houses at £100 each. After renovations, the property was converted to a night shelter with four bedsits on the first floor, a caretaker's apartment and a shop. While the project was underway, they organised a soup and sandwiches run to Cavan's Connolly Street car park each day at 10 p.m. for the benefit of the 'rolling stones' there.

When the night refuge was completed, they established an independent Conference – St Peter's – to run it. Even today, it is used by homeless men from all parts of Ireland and abroad. In recent times it has seen an increased demand for its amenities, which include a nourishing meal provided by SVP volunteers.

Fewer women find themselves homeless in the area, but those who do are accommodated in the local St Phelim's Hospital, known as the 'County Home'.

In time, the St Peter's Conference expanded and purchased further property, building a block of eight apartments, as well as buying some private houses – this at a time when the local urban council was unable to fully meet the demand for accommodation. 'However,' says Anselm Lovett, 'the SVP obtained government grants for the project on the condition that the accommodation would be for homeless people for at least thirty years.'

This ambitious Conference then embarked on the building of a large number of apartments (St Clare's Gardens) on property donated by the local Poor Clare Sisters. Eventually, the housing project became so large that it was decided to establish a new Conference – St Joseph's – to run it, leaving St Peter's with the sole responsibility of the homeless shelter. The St Joseph's Housing Conference now manages all of the Society's properties in Cavan and in February 2014, the magnificent Ozanam Centre was officially opened by President Michael D. Higgins in a premises just off Bridge Street.

Earlier, when a shop facing Bridge Street came up for sale it was bought by the Conference, who converted it into a Vincent's shop as well as additional accommodation. It is the proceeds of this very successful retail outlet that largely finance the demanding work of the night shelter.

Prior to the building of the night shelter, St Patrick's, the town's first Conference (established in 1860), decided to provide a halting site for Travellers on a site offered by the Sisters of St Clare. However, it was subsequently decided to leave that project to the local authority, who went ahead with it. A new Conference, Our Lady of the Wayside, was then formed to look after the needs of the Travellers. The Conference is still involved in that work, with financial support from St Patrick's.

The Day Dolores Struck a Low Note

Bill Lawlor

Occasionally, even the most accomplished and acclaimed personalities can fall victim to life's tribulations. One of these was internationally known Irish folk singer, Dolores Keane, to whom the Society of St Vincent de Paul rendered assistance in her time of need, after she had fought the demons of alcoholism and depression. She later fell ill with breast cancer, but has now been given the all-clear.

For many decades, the founding member of the successful group De Dannan has been a much-loved performer with Irish audiences, as well as those abroad. But as the years went by the demands and pressures of her professional career started to take their toll and it was in the late 1990s that she fell victim to the blues and the booze.

For the one-time contributor to the record-breaking album *A Woman's Heart*, a career of fame and even considerable fortune appeared to be over. A further calamity was a conviction for drink driving in December 2011, after which she entered Cuain Mhuire, the charitable drug, alcohol and gambling rehabilitation organisation, for treatment.

After coming out of that institution faced with financial problems and the task of supporting her children, she availed of the ready support of the SVP at the start of summer 2012.

Dolores lives with her two children near Headford, Co. Galway. Her marriage to musician John Faulkner ended in 1988. She says, 'My family had already done a great deal for me, including renovating my home to facilitate my son, Joseph, who has a sight problem. They also put in a new shower unit, re-tiled and redecorated the place. It was like going home to a new house. But I was stuck for money. At this stage I felt I had hit rock bottom.'

She made contact with the State-funded resource centre in Headford, where the local SVP Conference has a consulting room. She talked to the secretary of the amenity and shortly afterwards Dolores met Headford SVP Conference President Kevin Higgins, of whom she said, 'He was very helpful and he told me they would provide me with whatever help I required.'

Straight away she was given a mobile phone, a trailer of turf and food vouchers. She recalls that on many occasions throughout her career she had performed benefit concerts for charity organisations, including the SVP. She is aware that today there are many people availing of the Society's help who, like herself, thought they would never need to do so. Referring to seeking assistance, she says, 'If you need it you need it. Sometimes you need people like the St Vincent de Paul and you should never be ashamed to seek their help. Never mind what the people next door might think.'

She added, 'We have reached a stage now in Ireland when we must come down out of the clouds. Many people are too proud to admit their financial difficulties and seek aid. The help I got from the Vincent de Paul got me over my own personal financial difficulty at that time.'

Looking back on her recent success, the four-night run of the Woman's Heart concert in Dublin's Olympia Theatre, she adds: 'Without the help of Cuain Mhuire and the St Vincent de Paul I would not be where I am today.'

For SVP Conference President Kevin Higgins, who knew Dolores as a brilliant performer over many years, it was quite a shock to find the renowned award-winning singer seeking assistance. But he and his fellow Vincentians were more than willing to give whatever aid was required. He discovered that the 'very distressed' woman before him was 'penniless' and her partner had left their home. She was particularly concerned about looking after her son and daughter. He immediately organised the provision of food vouchers, but she also needed fuel, so the Conference discreetly arranged the delivery of a trailer-load of turf to her house, as well as giving her a mobile phone.

Says Kevin, 'As I talked to Dolores she poured out all her problems. She was in a very bad state and had obviously gone through a tough time. I wondered would she be able to get her life together again, and I said this to her. "Why wouldn't I?" she replied. She was very positive.'

He went on, 'The day I met her I was really sorry for her. I spent a good half an hour talking to her and I think she really appreciated it. She has her own house, but I don't think she had any immediate access to welfare benefits. Even though a five-member Conference like ours has limited resources, it is important that we are able to get people back on their feet again.' He points out that this was a case of getting someone over a temporary difficulty, which is a fairly regular task for the SVP.

Dolores also paid tribute to the Society, on RTÉ's The Late Late Show broadcast on 30 May 2014. 'They are brilliant people,' she said, and again recalled how the SVP had helped when times were difficult for her and her family.

'I wasn't ashamed or afraid. I went for help to the Society of St Vincent de Paul and they helped me out,' she told the show's presenter, Ryan Tubridy, who agreed with her that people in difficulties should not be reluctant to approach the SVP.

Here indeed is a woman of resilience, but also of humility, to whom the Society of St Vincent de Paul was happy to offer practical assistance.

Breffni: Youth for Justice – An Inspiring Concept

Bill Lawlor

A north-east family's days of austerity have been considerably eased by the initiative of transition year students from a secondary school in the region.

The teenage pupils' success in raising €1,800 to assist with the cost of running the household is a typical example of a Society of St Vincent de Paul-sponsored project, which has inspired young people to understand and take action on social justice issues.

The society's increasingly successful Youth for Justice programme, which commenced in 2002 in the SVP's Breffni Region (Sligo, North Mayo, Achonry and Leitrim), has been expanded to include the north-east (Meath, Louth, Cavan and Monaghan), Cork city and county, as well as the north-west (Inishowen, Dungloe, Letterkenny, Ardara, South Donegal, Convoy and Milford).

Sharon Tuohy, Breffni's youth development officer, points out that it provides second-level pupils with the opportunity to look at what's happening in their community and identify a need. They then develop a project to take action to help meet that need. She says, 'On my initial visit to a school, I speak to the students about the Society of St Vincent de Paul and the work of its members. Young people are often very surprised at the range of activity that SVP volunteers are involved with and the degree to which the issues encountered affect people's lives. This session is always a real eye-opener for students and ignites their passion to want to help in some way.'

Among the type of projects undertaken by schools are visits to nursing homes, hospitals, residential centres or reaching out to immigrant groups. She says they may also research and create awareness on a social issue and, through taking action, see how their work can affect social policy. In education projects, students set up and run homework and shared reading clubs to enhance learning opportunities for younger members of their communities.

Importantly, the youngsters also become involved in directly aiding the work of the Society by helping SVP members with their efforts. This may involve the creation and distribution of Christmas hampers, toy appeals or fundraising for local projects. 'Voluntary work can be very challenging, but the feelgood factor that comes from giving something of yourself to help someone in need is priceless,' adds Sharon. A highlight at the end of the school year for Youth for Justice participants is an annual exhibition of their work, where they celebrate and show their achievements to SVP members, fellow students and the general public.

So how did it all begin? Sharon recalls that when she commenced work with the SVP in 2001, she had a brief to focus her efforts on secondary schools. She then began looking at the possibilities of how she might engage this age group and encourage them to take on voluntary activity with the Society. She says, 'I initially ran some awareness-raising projects around the issue of poverty and the work of the SVP. This helped me to develop a good understanding of where the students were at and what their needs and interests were.

'At the time there was a woman working with SVP in Dublin – Anne Murphy. She was engaged with students in schools and running youth projects very successfully. I took lots of inspiration from Anne and began to adapt some of the projects she had been involved with to suit the needs of my groups.

'Slowly, the range and variety of projects in the region grew and eventually we had a thriving Youth for Justice programme in the schools in Breffni. Three years ago, the then SVP National President, Mairead Bushnell, attended our exhibition and was so impressed by the work on display that she asked that the Youth for Justice programme be rolled out around the country. So we undertook a project to document the work that I've been doing in the schools in my region and through this information we developed a manual to make it possible to replicate this work.'

After that, Attracta McNiece was appointed as development officer for the Society's north-east region, where a Youth for Justice pilot scheme was successfully run. The scheme has since been extended to two further SVP regions, Cork and the north-west, where the development officers are Susan Pearmain and Valerie Bryce, respectively. Sharon reports that these are 'going very well and we are looking to see how we can further replicate Youth for Justice around the country.'

Sharon has been consistently impressed by the range and diversity of student projects and by the creativity and motivation that has fired the young people's approach: 'Over the past ten years we in the Society have really been impressed by the students' innovation, commitment and genuine concern for the people they help,' she says, and adds, 'If these young people are our future, it's looking bright.'

She recalls that Frédéric Ozanam was only twenty when he founded the Society of St Vincent de Paul – 'not much older than many of the students I work with.'

'Youth for Justice is about harnessing the energy that young people possess and inspiring them to do great things,' she concludes.

Carne Holiday & Training Centre, Wexford

Joe Dalton

C arnsore Coastguard Station was built around 1940 to deal with sea emergencies in the south-east during wartime. It was handed over to the Society of St Vincent de Paul in the early 1950s to be used as the charity saw fit. It was renamed Carn Holiday Centre. A couple, Tony and Mary O'Rourke, were employed to run the centre.

Father Gaule, a Vincentian, brought many children from Dublin and the Wexford region to the centre on holidays over the next few years. Later on a new wing was added and less well-off families from all over Ireland were afforded a holiday at the centre.

All this time the centre was losing money. When Kitty Hynes became area president of Wexford in the early 2000s, she consulted with Regional Administrator David O'Neill to discuss the situation. It was decided the best course of action was to close the centre and formulate a plan of action for the future.

A Conference was formed around six months later. Its sole purpose was to rejuvenate the centre and make it fit for purpose for the diverse groups they anticipated would use it. St Martin's was the name of the new Conference, which consisted of thirteen members. It didn't take long for the Conference to set out a plan of action. Two of the members were involved in Scouts and Girl Guides. They encouraged these organisations to use Carne for their camping holidays, which they did and are doing to this day in large numbers. This, along with a large number of diverse groups using the centre, allows Carne to cater for the less well-off families in our society and still make a profit for the SVP.

Situated on the beautiful coastline of the south-east corner of Ireland, Carne Holiday & Training Centre (HTC) offers everything needed for a residential weekend or a camp. Located within ten yards of the rugged but safe coastline, Carne HTC offers the most splendid of accommodation, facilities and natural amenities.

Carne HTC can offer indoor accommodation for up to sixty-three people in the main house with adjacent cottage accommodation for up to twelve people. Cottages are close enough to be used for leader and staff accommodation. Rooms are available for one, two, three and four persons, all equipped with sinks and hot and cold water. They include an ensuite leaders' room for three persons. Camping is available on various sites around the house, with access to toilets and showers. There is also a wet weather shelter available for use by campers.

They also offer a modern, fully equipped self-catering kitchen which conforms to all health standards, along with two coffee docks off the training room. There is a large dining room which can accommodate up to eighty people, along with a private staff dining room. Carne hosts a large training/Conference room with three additional areas that can be used if needed.

Carne is situated twenty-five minutes' drive from Wexford town and within twenty minutes of cinema and bowling. Group prices can be arranged on request. The Centre is ten minutes' drive from Rosslare Ferry port, with easy access to Wales, the UK and France. Available train stations are Wexford or Rosslare. Canoeing can be arranged on request and there are many coastal walks along with horse riding nearby and, of course, the wonderful sweeping beaches which have lifeguards at high season. Lifeguards can also be sourced for off-season activities.

For information contact the centre by email: carneholidaycentre@yahoo.ie

St Joseph's Housing Development, Gorey, Co. Wexford

Edmund Roche

The Christian Brothers owned a wonderful monastery with a beautiful garden space and a secondary school adjacent to it, about one minute's walk from the main street of Gorey.

The Gorey Conference had been using the old science room of the Christian Brothers School for a few years as their local clothes outlet. When the Conference heard that the Brothers were selling the monastery and school in 1999, they decided to make an offer to the Brothers to purchase the science rooms, which were separate from the main school. However, the Brothers wished to sell everything in one lot rather than divide portions of it for sale. Their asking price for the monastery, gardens and school in 1999 was the equivalent of €635,000. The Conference was faced with a challenge they never anticipated. How could they raise the money needed to buy the entire lot? And not only buy it, but renovate the monastery, which needed major restoration work if it was going to be used by the public?

Enter Wexford County Council. With the cooperation of the council, St Joseph's Conference was able to enter into negotiations to get planning permission and funding for the development of a housing scheme. This scheme would eventually consist of fourteen houses built on the monastery garden and six apartments in the monastery itself. Some of the funding came from the Social Housing Programme.

The Gorey Conference had to sell some property they already owned in Gorey in order to raise their share of the costs. Finally, we were able to purchase the monastery, gardens and school as one lot for less than the asking price. We paid the equivalent of €622,300 for the property. The St Vincent de Paul head office gave us a loan equivalent to €122,000 to help us make the purchase.

It was essential to maintain the original structure of the monastery. With careful planning and design, this was possible. We managed to retain all the original flooring throughout the building. We also retained the original reception rooms and the original chapel. A new kitchen had to be built as well as a new and larger dining area to facilitate all residents. Shortly after the project was completed in 2005, the housing scheme won a national architectural award.

With the help of FÁS, we are able to employ a caretaker and three kitchen staff to provide meals and housekeeping assistance to all our residents. The caretaker deals with repairs and the upkeep of the grounds as well as helping the residents with any gardening needs they may have.

All the houses and apartments are redecorated by professional decorators every two years, or sooner if there is a change of tenant.

New St Vincent de Paul Hostel for Waterford

Gordon Power

Since it was acquired by the Society in 1947, the Lady Lane Men's Hostel is not only one of the main focal points of the SVP in the south-east region, but has also become a local Waterford landmark. The Lady Lane Hostel is funded in partnership by the SVP, Waterford City Council and the HSE. Originally established as a soup kitchen, it went on to provide short-term accommodation for homeless men. The needs of homeless men have changed a great deal since its inception and the old dormitories have since been replaced by private rooms and specially trained project workers are provided to give the men one-to-one assistance. Project workers are qualified in the social field and provide many levels of support, helping the men to link in with other local services and giving them the direction to get a home of their own and move on to independent living.

Dignity and Respect

Over the past ten years, it has become apparent that the needs of homeless men have again changed. The Lady Lane Hostel has been modernised and improved, but despite this it became obvious that to maintain the hostel's reputation for excellence we needed to start again from a custom-built facility. So began the planning process under the direction of the regional president, Terence O'Neill, the area president, Larry Roche, and the regional administrator, Ray McDonald. The site of Bath Street was acquired specifically with this in mind. It was purchased with the benefit of money bequeathed to us by the McGwire fund. As an homage to this benevolent man and his family, it has been decided that the new hostel will be called McGwire House. The name does not contain the word 'hostel'. This has been done intentionally as we do not want residents to feel stigmatised or demoralised about having to use a homeless facility.

Historically, many people who would have used a hostel would have had alcohol or addiction issues. Today, the demographic of men who use the service has totally changed. With the deterioration of the national economy, rise in unemployment and breakdown of family units, many men who do not have addiction or mental health issues find themselves homeless and in need of the support of a homeless hostel. McGwire House, although providing the service of a homeless hostel, will not feel like one. Each resident will have access to his own modern, specially designed private room, many of which also have their own private toilet and shower room. McGwire House will be Ireland's most modern hostel and will be one of the SVP's flagship facilities in Ireland. The quality of the build was paramount in the building process, which is why BAM Building Ltd, with many large projects under its belt, was finally chosen to complete the build.

A New Home

McGwire House will provide more than a roof for these men. It has been designed to feel like a home. It has always been the ethos of Lady Lane Hostel to treat all its residents with dignity and respect. This has always been in line with the basic fundamental sentiments of the Society of the St Vincent de Paul and history has shown us that giving a man back these traits is one of the first major steps in getting them back to independent living. The excellent reputation and work ethic of the staff has been developed over many years. The Lady Lane Hostel is staffed by healthcare professionals, who work alongside members of the FÁS Community Employment Schemes. Over the years, this scheme has given many people the advantage of working in this industry, receiving relevant training and accreditation to help them move on to full-time employment.

The Changing Needs of the Homeless

One major aspect of the design of McGwire House is the change of thinking around the needs of homeless men. Many men are unable to maintain independent living because they lack what many would assume to be some very basic living skills. Some residents become homeless for a second or third time because of something as simple as being unable to budget to save for rent or even being able to prepare basic meals. To cater for this need, Lady Lane Hostel has successfully run the Life Skills Programme. This has identified the particular needs of men on an individual basis and programmes are specifically designed to cater for these particular requirements. Men have been helped with literacy skills, basic food preparation, fiscal planning and in many other ways. McGwire House will also provide a designated area for this life skills training. This area has its own kitchen and special training area, which will help the residents to develop the skills they need to attain and maintain independent living.

Another major need identified was something to occupy the men's time. Many of the residents are unemployed and time can weigh heavily upon them. McGwire House has acquired a substantial amount of land at the rear of the property and it is intended over time to develop this area into gardens and also to grow vegetables and produce which can be used in the McGwire House kitchens. It has also been proposed to provide a gym for the men, as in addition to these concerns, the health of the residents is paramount and anything that can be provided to increase their health and foster healthy living is a bonus.

Many suggestions have been made relating to the future of 18 Lady Lane. A committee consisting of Mary O'Brien, Con O'Riordan, John Caulfield and Terence O'Neill has been formed under the area president, Margaret Conway. This committee is looking at a number of options to maximise the use of the building within the area in the future.

McGwire House will serve as a centre of excellence and as a model to highlight the best treatment, practices and care for homeless men. One of the greatest abilities of the Lady Lane Hostel was to transform and meet the ever-changing needs of homeless men and McGwire House will continue to do so for many years to come and carry on the principles and ethos of the Society of St Vincent de Paul.

Integration – Intégration – Integracijos

Joe Dalton

*I*ntegration is the opportunity afforded to all to be part of and contribute to mainstream society.

There was a large influx of people from all continents to Ireland around 2000. These included migrant workers, refugees and asylum seekers. As members of St Vincent de Paul, we saw it as a challenge and an opportunity to help these people with the transition of coming from other cultures and adapting to the Irish lifestyle.

An integration programme was designed and developed and brought into play in 2001. With the blessing of the then Waterford area president and area treasurer, Larry Roche and Anne Waters, the first integration workshop took place in May of that year. Together, local families and new communities attended and through discussion, games and the arts they shared their life experiences and their visions for the future. The new communities enjoyed this greatly as it afforded them a direct opportunity of contact with locals in a safe, friendly environment.

Later that year, along with the support of auxiliary members, we set up weekly integration workshops in Birchwood Refugee Centre, Waterford. This was also based on sharing, as in the above programme. On different weeks, invited guests from the local area would attend and share their talents – from music to art to dancing, etc. It gave the residents an opportunity to see what the Irish lifestyle was like.

Barbecues were held during the summer at different venues – Kilfarrissey Beach, Holy Family Church grounds and Edmund Rice International Heritage Centre, Barrack Street, Waterford. These events were eagerly looked forward to as they were a platform for the sharing of all types of food, singing, dancing and chit-chat.

We've all heard the story of the 'loaves and fishes'. Well, at our barbecue on Kilfarrissey Beach, we had the story of the 'missing halal chickens and the fresh mackerels'.

To cater for the Muslim section of the 150 people in attendance, six fresh halal chickens were purchased for the event. However, when we all arrived and inspected the supplies, it became obvious that we had overlooked the chickens. A large stock of burgers and sausages were ready for the 'barbie', but not a chicken was in sight for our Muslim friends. Well, it just so happened that one of our group was down at the water's edge chatting to a man fishing – a German who lives in Kilkenny. When he heard our predicament, this German graciously offered us the thirty fresh mackerel he had caught that evening. So in the end all were fed and satisfied with the fare.

The integration barbecues continue to take place every year in the grounds of the Edmund Rice International Heritage Centre. We are very grateful for the continuing support the Brothers give us.

Adult and Teenage Integration

In 2002 it was decided to create separate adult and teenage integration sections. This gave more focus to the needs of the individual age groups. The adult section took place weekly in the meeting room of the Holy Family Church. This section ran for four years and was of great benefit to all who attended.

Teenage Integration blossomed at a great pace. Teenagers were eager to meet their peers, discuss issues relevant to their age, and to share and learn from one another's sharing. On average, Teenage Integration workshops took place once a fortnight and there was an attendance of thirty plus at each session. This continued for quite a few years with the help of so many auxiliary members.

In 2009 it was noticed that natural integration had come into play, with the new community teenagers engaged in schools, local clubs and societies in our area. It was decided to cease the workshops at this stage as we had achieved our aims.

The following are the thoughts of some of the teenagers who took part in the integration programme over the years.

Cecilia Liu

'I am a loving person,' that is one of the most important things I have learned from Teenage Integration. Being a loving person means accepting myself first as an individual, accepting my personal quirks and progressing to love others around me. I was a shy teenager then; simple things such as talking in front of a small group of people were a challenge. Slowly but surely, I developed the confidence to overcome this and from then on, I walk with confidence every day. Seven years on, I still walk by this motto. I also met my best friend, who is one of the most important people in my life, thanks to Teenage Integration.

Eniola Oladiti

Teenage Integration was the place to be. It was packed with loads of fun and amazing people. I attended the sessions for quite a few years and I must say I thoroughly enjoyed it. Teenage Integration was a real friendly place; it had people from all different countries, races and ages. We learned about other cultures and religious beliefs by working together on various projects. There was always a range of fun-filled activities and of course snacks to keep us going for the duration of the programme. Every now and then we were taken on tours to different places to help us explore and increase our knowledge, such as the reptile zoo in Gowran. You were sure to have made a new friend before the end of the trip. What made Teenage Integration fantastic is that it was filled with teenagers who could relate to each other on different topics and also enjoy each other's company playing the diverse games at the sessions.

Eoin White

I first got involved with the Integration group after it was suggested to me by some friends at the time. As I was doing nothing outside of my school hours, I thought it might be a useful way to spend my time other than homework and study. Some people thought that it was rather out of character for me to get involved with something like this, but I still attended the first group meeting, albeit with some restraint. At first I did not know what to expect, but after the first week I could not wait to return.

I was introduced to many different people from a variety of backgrounds. As I was a naturally shy person, I was certain that I would not speak or get involved at the beginning. I could not have been more wrong. From the beginning, everyone was encouraged to get involved, and some were given an extra push to make themselves known and before I knew it, everyone was talking and giving their input into the group. We had large group discussions on many topics, and each person shared their view. No one was penalised or scolded if their views differed from that of the group, which was very refreshing.

The group engaged in meditation and other relaxing activities that, even though they were alien to me, were genuinely helpful, especially with all of the stresses of school such as exams, which I had found cumbersome at the time. Each activity was designed so that everybody had equal input and everyone was encouraged to speak up if they had any comments or ideas on activities.

As the weeks progressed, we really became a tight-knit group of friends whose friendships went beyond just Integration, as we all genuinely appreciated each other and were interested in what we thought or felt. There were also other activities such as origami and mock duels, which were all a lot of fun. Even after Integration had ended, I still engaged in some of the activities that interested me in order to keep my skills up and also because it was very fun.

Most of the friends that I made in the Integration group stayed with me all through secondary school and into my university years. At the time I also introduced them to my school friends, and they all go out and have a great time even to this day. Even though I have lost contact with some of the people from the group now, I have no doubt that if we were to see each other in the street, we would act as if no time had passed, as we all truly appreciated each other for who we are.

My time with the Integration group was without a doubt very well spent. It was a great way to spend an evening and without it I would not have a sense of self-appreciation and confidence that factors into my decisions even to this day.

Dion Chan

Teenage Integration was a friendly, positive and energetic place where teenagers of all ages felt safe and free to express their opinions. In this environment, each individual could bring out their uniqueness while meeting and socialising with new people. Here they were not judged by their background, culture, religion or colour of their skin. It felt rewarding to assist creative activities and support and witness the transformation of shy teenagers coming out of their shells and making friends. I also benefited by engaging and being a part of a group of fun-loving, genuine and caring people who prove that no matter what age or ethnicity, there's a child in all of us.

Combined Teenage Celebration

A progression of Teenage Integration was the formation of the Combined Teenage Celebration. In 2009, secondary schools in the south-east were approached and invited to put together a programme for sharing by their students. It was desirable that the group would reflect the diverse cultural mix in the schools. All groups came together in Edmund Rice Chapel, Barrack Street, Waterford in February of that year, where they shared their musical and dancing abilities. Two hundred students from fifteen schools took part in the first gathering and what was profound was that all who attended performed at the event. Damien Tiernan, south-east correspondent with RTÉ, was MC for the occasion. This in itself elevated the event in the teenagers' eyes as it was brought to the attention of such a wide audience when they appeared on national television.

This is an ongoing event which is eagerly looked forward to by both the students and their music teachers. As one music teacher commented, 'It is brilliant for the students as there is no pressure on them as it is not a competition – but a sharing.'

Combined Teenage Celebration – A Great Idea

Damien Tiernan

As RTÉ south-east correspondent, I get asked to speak or get involved in maybe two dozen or so events each year in the region, many of which I have to decline due to work commitments, etc. But when Joe Dalton came to me with details of the Combined Choirs Celebration, I was immediately hooked.

In my line of work, over the years I have covered many stories, both good and bad. Racism is one of those which turns my stomach most; I abhor it and everything that goes with it. I have also been deeply involved with the National Union of Journalists for many years and our Code of Conduct is very specific on this, with section 9 stating: 'A journalist should produce no material likely to lead to hatred or discrimination on the grounds of a person's age, gender, race, colour, creed, legal status, disability, marital status or sexual orientation.'

The idea of young people coming together in a joyous celebration of music and song under the banner of the St Vincent de Paul was something that greatly appealed to me – so much so that when I was compèring the event at the lovely Mount Sion Chapel, I took a day's annual leave to make sure I was going to be there!

And the extent of the talent on show was superb. From the 'brush dancers' from the Mercy in Waterford to the vivaciousness of YouthReach in Waterford to the drummers and percussionists from the CBS in New Ross to the traditional musicians from Scoil Mhuire in Carrick-on-Suir: all magnificent in their own right. It is so great to see so many schools from around the south-east coming together to learn from each other and share experiences and make new friends. Yeats College, Mount Sion, Newtown and De La Salle all also had superb youngsters brave enough to get up on stage and perform in front of their peers – some for the very first time. And it's not about competition, as Joe rightly set out when he started this event, it's about celebration of diversity, of different creeds and beliefs and races; it's about everybody with one purpose trying to make the world a better place by starting with the simple things.

I remember saying one of the most important things to do as teenagers is not to send or resend racist text messages if someone sends one 'as a joke' – to reply, saying you are against this sort of thing. And to follow that up, when someone at school tells a racist joke in a group and everyone is supposed to laugh, be brave and tell them it's not funny and to cop on. It's sometimes a very hard thing to do but it's in little moments like that when real character is developed and leaders emerge.

Well done to all those who have taken part and continue to take part in this excellent event and I hope I'll be asked back again! Well done to Joe and all those that organise the event, to those in the Brother Rice Centre, to the school teachers and pupils especially. And well done to the St Vincent de Paul for supporting this most worthy of causes. Long may it continue and flourish. And a massive congrats to all those who continue to work tirelessly for the charity in this very important year of celebration.

Thank you!

Adeola Awodele

For the past few years I have been invited to the annual programme in Edmund Rice Chapel, Barrack Street, Waterford. To tell the truth I have had an amazing experience in each gathering.

People of different ages, sizes and races gather together to share their feelings through music, be it through voice, dance or instruments. Instruments range from violin to guitar to tin whistle to bagpipes. Programmes such as these allow people to socialise with others; people often leave with a new friend's phone number, email address or Facebook name. There is never a dull moment and of course there is always a snack at the end for us hungry teenagers and to be honest we often refuse to leave due to the fact that we are having too much fun. Talking about it now makes me excited for the upcoming programme next year.

Bringing Quilted Unity to a Prison

Bulletin Extract

Cloverhill Prison Visitors' Centre is a purpose-built modern building attached to Cloverhill Remand Prison, which has capacity for 430 prisoners in Clondalkin, Dublin.

The centre is operated by the Dublin Region of the SVP and the Society of Friends and was opened in 2000. It caters for 78,000 adults and children per year.

The ethos of Cloverhill Prison Visitors' Centre is to provide a safe, pleasant, friendly and supportive environment to those visiting family members and friends in Cloverhill Remand Prison. Services include a free tea/coffee/snack bar service, a fully equipped childcare/play area, parenting advice and support, family support, an information and advocacy service and a volunteer programme. A number of children's arts and crafts projects are run, as many children who avail of the childcare services have very little contact, if any, with projects in their local areas. This is usually as a result of the financial implications faced by many when a family member is sent to prison.

'We wanted to devise an activity that could be accessed by children on an ad hoc basis,' a centre organiser said. 'Some children spend a considerable amount of time with

144

us while others are here for short periods of time only. We needed to come up with something that all children could participate in and just as importantly see the end result. The idea of a patchwork quilt was suggested by one of the childcare workers. Children could work on patches while in the centre but if time was limited they could bring a patch home with them to complete.'

Seventy-six children worked on the patchwork quilt either in the centre or at home. Adults also got involved and parents and guardians worked on the patches with their children or completed their own while in the centre or at home on their own time. A number of prison and courthouse staff were also involved, with the result being that by the time the quilt was complete, everyone connected to Cloverhill Prison Visitors' Centre had contributed in some way.

To reflect this, the patchwork quilt has been called 'Unity': the state of being one, or united.

From Revolution to Shopping – Using Everything

Bulletin Extract

S ean McDermott Street has seen a lot of Irish history: revolution, strikes, depression, poverty and recovery and it is where the Society of St Vincent de Paul has its national headquarters and its biggest charity shop in Dublin. 'We Reuse it All' is the slogan of the shops, which are now a vital part of consumer support and a social outreach to those in need from the Society.

Five million people visit SVP shops in Dublin every year. The thirty-four Vincent's retail outlets in the Dublin region are part of a major outreach by the Society to the public and a fundraising operation which helps to provide the financial resources needed by those who approach the Society for assistance.

There are more than 150 SVP shops nationwide. 'SVP shops are more than just shops, they provide a vital service in the community,' says Dermot McGilloway, regional manager of retail services in the SVP Dublin region. 'They are a contact point for the Society, they distribute information,

146

they are a presence in the community, indicating that the SVP is there to help.'

New initiatives are regularly introduced and one in Dublin attracted a lot of attention – the first SVP wedding shop! The Bridal Wear and Special Occasions shop opened at 92 Terenure Road North on a floor above the existing Vincent's shop. With the average wedding dress costing between €700 and €1,500, this service will be of considerable help to those planning weddings,' said McGilloway. 'After the "big day", bridal gowns and other wedding attire, including unwanted gifts, can be donated to the SVP, providing help for others; this is what we are about, helping those who need our assistance.'

Dermot McGilloway's office in the Dublin SVP regional base at Sean McDermott Street in the heart of Dublin city centre is above the SVP region's main store, which is a busy place. Behind the public face of the shop is a busy warehouse centre where clothes and other items donated to the SVP are brought for initial examination, sorting and preparation for resale. Vans collect from the thirty-four shops in the region and deliver to Sean McDermott Street, where they are then recycled and prepared for reuse, after they have been sorted and treated. A wide variety of additional items as well as clothing are donated and every one is carefully checked for future usage. The variety of donated items is wide ranging. The store has glassware, souvenir items, postage stamps, jewellery, books, videos and much else besides. As well as the wide range of clothing and accessories, there are household items, books, toys, collectibles and antiques. This resource provides the wide variety of choice offered to customers in Vincent's shops. The shops themselves are impressive. They are well laid out, with clothing and other items nicely displayed, a regular retail presentation, the response to which has been strong customer support.

'There are now thirty-four separate locations in the Dublin region and there is a lot of variety and choice,' Dermot McGilloway says. 'Lucan has a new shop and a dedicated bookshop, for example. All of the shops are providing a vital service in the community. They are a public face for the Society of St Vincent de Paul at the heart of thirty-four communities in Dublin. They distribute information on SVP services in eleven languages and information on homeless and other services which the Society provides. Our shops provide emergency assistance for homeless visitors who cannot avail of Conference assistance at that time and who can then be referred as needed for more help. They provide social interaction, which is important between customers, SVP volunteers and shop staff, in a welcoming environment and we operate a policy of running customer appreciation evenings to show how much the SVP values the support we receive.'

The system developed in the Dublin region has been devised by constant study and assessment of the needs of customers, driven by the main purpose of the Society, which is not to operate a retail sales business, but a service which helps those in need in the widest, most efficient and responsive way, at the core of which is the recycling of unwanted items donated by the public.

'This is our unique way of recycling, or reusing. We say and we mean it, that "at St Vincent de Paul we reuse it all."' The Vincent's shops are totally committed to recycling and ensure that every single garment donated to the SVP in the Dublin region is either given out under our emergency assistance programme, sold, or further recycled. All must be used in the maximum way to do what was intended by the donor and that is to provide support for those in need through the Society. 'We have a great team, volunteers and staff who are dedicated in the commitment they give to this work. Our warehouse team found a market for unsold bric-a-brac and household items. The warehouse also recycles cardboard and plastic. Our team goes to exceptional lengths to extract the maximum value out of all donated goods and are committed to continuous improvement in the areas of pollution prevention, waste reduction and the reuse, recovery and recycling of every donated item.'

As well as donations coming from the Vincent's shops, other collection points are regularly in place at churches, in addition to company and mobile collections. Clothing is the predominant item donated, but Vincent's has now diversified with a much wider range of goods on sale, such as jewellery, books, CDs, toys and cards.

SVP's 'Donate with Style' campaign was successfully developed and the Society has worked hard to widen its reach in attracting donations. The society holds collection points not only at Catholic churches but across a number of religious denominations – a move that has received tremendous support. Vincent's shops offer a unique proposition to the community: under one roof, a homeless person can avail of clothing for free in line with its charitable ethos while at the same time designer items can also be purchased.

'The Vincent's line of shops have become steadily more profitable, enjoying seven to eight years of sustained growth, providing the Society with a net contribution of €2 million this year. This incremental growth has sprung from a cultural transformation, with changes taking place in the running of the shops. The new approach focuses on emphasising quality, allowing Vincent's to be run like a business while staying true to its charitable ethos,' said Dermot McGilloway.

There is a Great Lunch in Rathmullan

On the northernmost point of Donegal, right up on the Foyle Estuary, a coach arrives and people get off, head into the bright, cream-coloured building and begin to talk, drink tea and coffee, discuss the current news and then settle in for a day's activities. A cold grey November morning, a warm early spring day, they come from many parts of Donegal to the SVP Rathmullan Social Centre, where the building is constructed on a site donated by Donegal County Council.

The morning is a busy one at the centre, staffed by a full-time manager/cook, assisted by a number of part-time FÁS and Rural Social Scheme participants as well as local SVP volunteers. Wednesday and Thursday are the particularly busy days, with the HSE providing a grant to the SVP St Joseph's Social Works Conference to help run the centre.

In the big sitting room on a winter's morning there is a comfortable fire, the newspapers, magazines and books are out, and there is lots of chatter. There are many elderly people for whom these are the days when they meet people, when loneliness is replaced by social connection and also the days to learn things. There is a computer class, there are

150

physical exercises, there is lunch, there is time to relax, to meet and talk. It is a 'home from home' is what its regulars say, a place where the local community has taken the SVP and its work to heart.

Uniting the Generations in Galway

Bulletin Extract

L oneliness and isolation are key social issues which have been responded to by the Society of St Vincent de Paul in Galway City at the resource centre, Croí Na Gaillimhe, whose work is focused on human caring and consideration.

'We cannot underestimate the power of touch, a smile, a kind word, a listening ear, an honest compliment, or the smallest act of caring, all of which have the potential to turn life around,' says the centre manager, Loretta Needham. 'Loneliness and isolation are highlighted in numerous reports as key issues for older people and for society in general. This must be of concern to us all, no matter what walk of life we are from.'

The centre facilitates integration of people across all cultural, social and economic divides, offering a social club to older people and educational and developmental supports for youths and adults. Having an SVP resource centre in Galway provides the foundation from which the integration of local communities can develop. As well as the social club, a range of activities take place in the centre, such as computer training, drawing classes, movement and relaxation classes, line dancing, creative writing courses, a knitting club, tea dances, training for transformation, looking at the economy through women's eyes, life skills training and the Living Scenes intergenerational programme.

Working with other organisations and groups, including NUI Galway, Galway Community College and others, valuable research and development has been carried out at Croí Na Gaillimhe, such as with older clients on the Living Scenes intergenerational project.

'The focus of the centre is on positively impacting the lives of people through empowering, enabling and relationship building in a specifically designed learning environment which allows groups to develop, bond and form new relationships and friendships,' said Loretta.

SVP Conference of St James President Jim Harrington, who was involved with the creation of the centre, said that its development was achieved 'in consultation with several voluntary and statutory bodies in Galway which highlighted the need for a city-centre facility, catering for the needs of older people and providing a number of supports for young people.'

The centre was made possible due to the bequest of the late Maureen O'Connell to the SVP, which transformed a building at Mill Street that was in very poor condition into Croí na Gaillimhe.

Young at Heart

Briege Stevens and Kevin Cooley

Conference, area, regional and national St Vincent de Paul meetings are often sidetracked by discussions about how, and often whether or not, young people should be recruited to the SVP. The ideal that 'the youth are the future of the SVP' is, for most Conferences, an aspiration that is regularly talked about but never acted upon.

In 2006, one of the north-west's smaller border village Conferences in the heart of Donegal acknowledged that there was a need to answer the 'questionable' call from students in its local secondary school for extra tuition and after-school grinds. Funds needed to be raised to provide grinds, so members of the Little Flower Conference made contact with the school's principal and were directed towards English teacher and historian, Mr Jimmy Keogh.

Mr Keogh's aim for this project was that if it were to be successful and for the students involved to have the motivation to see it through to the end, it must have a fun element to it. Armed with Dictaphones and cameras, students from six classes in Choláiste Cholmcille, Ballyshannon, began their research by interviewing older people in their community and collected a catalogue of poems and factual articles.

The material produced by the students was so impressive that Mr Keogh had the idea to publish it in the form of a book, and the prospect of having their work published and recognised within the community was welcomed enthusiastically by the school.

Funding was required to print the book, so a dance organised by parents of the students involved in the project overcame that obstacle. Local man Ted Hall then conceived the idea that the book and its accompanying CD be launched by the Australian Ambassador to Ireland. For a small village the occasion of the arrival of such a dignitary created much excitement among the students and a truly memorable evening was had by everyone who attended the launch. Every student that contributed to the book was presented with a certificate on the night from the ambassador, but the certificate was only a symbol of what was really presented to these students when they became involved.

St Vincent de Paul volunteers throughout Ireland are all too aware of the belief of many of its members that 'the nature of SVP work is changing.' The outcomes of this project and the foresight of the members of the Little Flower Conference in Pettigo demonstrates that the future of community spirit in our towns and villages can rely on youth to take over from long-standing members.

The certificate presented on the launch night of *Pettigo – A Border Village in the Heart of Donegal* to the young individuals represents the students' achievement. This experience should change the belief of some SVP members that projects like this are either not worth pursuing or supporting with time or financial resources.

Trusting young people with the reins of the Society of St Vincent de Paul in order to steer it in the direction it needs to go is what experienced members need to do now. Investing in the recruitment of young people to SVP is

155

our only hope of understanding the problems that young families and individuals are experiencing now. Believing that the problems we experienced growing up are the problems people are living with now is an assumption that is failing to attract the people who at present don't approach the SVP for assistance and yet are in the most need of help.

Entrusting the young members in our Conferences with the responsibility of becoming the next president or treasurer is an ideal that should not only be aspired to but acted upon now. It is our only hope of making a significant positive impact on the new problems communities are facing today.

Sales of the book and CD produced by the students of Coláiste Cholmcille amounted to €1,200 and a cheque was presented to Little Flower Conference. Grinds and extra tuition were made available to local students. So, a problem *for* young people was addressed and solved *by* young people. Who would have thought?

Shine On Sunshine

Bulletin Extract

*L*iving conditions in Dublin's slums of the 1920s and 1930s were notoriously poor, overcrowded, unsanitary, dark and dangerous. Children were disproportionately affected, with infant mortality high, tuberculosis and measles rife and malnutrition common, so much so that the death rate resembled that of Calcutta.

SVP Conferences were overwhelmed by the needs of families throughout the capital. Simultaneously, a number of local youth clubs tried to cater for the burgeoning population of children by organising activities, sports and educational programmes.

In 1928, a group of SVP members decided to provide holidays away from the city as a means of giving young people sunshine, nutritious food and time to play and be children. They formed the Conference of the Infant Jesus of Prague, better known today as the Sunshine Fund.

After initially providing holidays and day trips, including to Gormanstown Strand, the success of their efforts led to the issuing of the *Advocate* newspaper to raise funds, backed by a church gate collection that raised an initial £300, which was a lot of money at the time, and Loughlinstown Hospital provided a disused wing for the first week's holiday ever held.

Soon after, Rochfort House, a former Church of Ireland rectory in Balbriggan, north Dublin, became available and was renamed Sunshine House. With upgrading and the addition of new facilities over the years, even overcoming the ration books of World War II, the years passed and the slums were cleared, but the need for Sunshine House remained. Today, it still provides as strong a service as ever with 100,000 children now having been catered for by teams of SVP volunteers.

'There are a million things that Sunshine House does for children, they have a great time and talk about it and make friends for years.' Those are the type of rewards which Sunshine helps to shine.

Belfast's Vincentian Education Fund

Bill Lawlor

Financial assistance towards the cost of further education is traditionally one of the greatest demands made upon the Society of St Vincent de Paul. It was not surprising, therefore, that the receipt in 2001 of a financial bequest by the North Belfast Area Conference resulted in a decision to use part of it to help with the provision of third-level study for needy students in the area. The decision was greatly influenced by the perceived importance in everyone's life of continuing training and also by an awareness that quite a number of young people were abandoning their tuition for economic reasons.

The Vincentian Education Fund was established following the formation of a committee to investigate and initiate the project. It advances the education of people of all denominations and none who live in north Belfast – the area comprising the SVP's North Belfast Area Council.

A total of thirty-six students have benefited to date. Beneficiaries must pursue a full-time course of study at a recognised college, university or college of further education, leading to the attainment of a foundation degree, higher national diploma, or primary degree. The determination of grant eligibility depends on the applicants' financial needs, family circumstances and record of educational achievement. An award is usually paid to the successful candidates for the duration of their course, subject to the production of satisfactory evidence of success in the required examinations.

The year 2001–2002 was the first in which students benefited from the scheme. Only a small number of applications were received up to 2008, and twelve students each received grants of £800 a year for their courses. However, since 2008 there has been a considerable increase in demand for grants. In 2011–2012, twenty-four people, including nine new applicants – who are at various stages in their study schedules – received grants.

In 2009 it was decided to increase the grant total to £1,200 a year for people studying in Northern Ireland, and £1,500 for those pursuing courses in England, Scotland, Wales and the Republic of Ireland. The sums are paid in three amounts, usually in September, January and April.

During the academic year 2011-2012, £31,200 was spent.

St Colman's Youth Conference, Carrick-on-Suir

Brendan McCarthy

S t Colman's Youth Conference was founded by Noel
Casey as part of a religion class, in the Christian Brothers'
Secondary School on St Colman's Feast Day, 24 November
1971. With over forty members, it is one of the few Youth
Conferences affiliated to the Society of St Vincent de Paul
in Ireland. The Conference is also a member of the Carrick-
on-Suir St Vincent de Paul Area Council, which brings six
Conferences from local and surrounding areas together.
Former Youth Conference President Barry Lonergan is the
president of the area council.

If you ask any member of this Youth Conference about
the most anticipated date in their Conference calendar, you
will most likely hear 'The Toy Appeal'. St Colman's Youth
Conference is best known for the Christmas Toy Appeal,
as it is one of the Conference's most successful and public
operations. Our annual Toy Mass is the highlight of this
appeal. The Toy Mass takes place every December, in St
Nicholas' Church. Toys are offered by generous givers at
the Mass, and the remainder are purchased with the various
donations the Conference receives throughout the year.

Donations of toys are also greatly appreciated from various organisations such as Scoil Mhuire Greenhill Secondary School, and the CBS Secondary School. This Mass is very special indeed as Santa Claus himself visits Carrick-on-Suir earlier than Christmas Eve, to thank all the boys and girls who have kindly donated gifts.

The work taken on by the Conference has been interesting, challenging, and at times frustrating to begin with, but always satisfying to finish. This Conference is quite different to the senior SVP Conferences in that it does not deal with home visitation and helping of disadvantaged families financially. A more hands-on approach is taken, especially when working with the elderly. We organise six senior citizen parties per year, which accommodate up to eighty senior citizens; this is the main activity during the year. These parties are generously sponsored by local groups such as the Credit Union, Social Services Committee, and the senior SVP Conferences, with the remainder sponsored by the youth Conference from funding received. Each year a coach tour is organised in the summer by the Conference for 100 senior citizens. The distribution of meals on wheels is also assisted by the Conference on a weekly basis, and in the past, house painting, gardening and hospital visitation have all taken place. A new Conference activity is a cinema club in Brewery Lane, Carrick-on-Suir. The films shown have included *The Sound of Music* and *The Quiet Man*. The senior citizens who attend enjoy these films greatly.

Due to an ever-increasing membership, the consistent aim of the Conference is to broaden its work. All members' suggestions are encouraged, along with suggestions from those outside the Conference.

In 2009, an SVP Youth Camp took place in Salamanca, Spain. This camp was the official international youth camp of the SVP and it recognised the active involvement of young people within the Society. It is hoped that young people will become more involved as at present the Society lacks the input of young volunteers in many countries. St Colman's Youth Conference is almost unique as one of the very few youth Conferences in Ireland.

St Colman's would like to help devise and co-operate in a national youth forum in the future, if it can get the support of the national organisers of the Society. They intend to get young people together to share ideas and develop the youth side of the Society. In the case of St Colman's, the Youth Conference has proven to be beneficial not only for those who have been on the receiving end of its philanthropy but also for the members themselves. It appears that the work and selflessness practised has actually developed members socially and heightened their understanding of the surrounding environment. This is due to the tireless work and advice given by Noel Casey, the founder, who is still an active member today.

New members from the age of fifteen and upwards are always welcome. Meetings are held every Friday at 7 p.m. in the Heritage Centre. Also, if you are involved in any other organisations or causes and you would like to get us involved or help out in any way, please contact us; as we have mentioned, we need to expand our work activities. Be involved in something unique, give a little and the Conference will give you back a lot more.

Cooperation is the Watchword in Donegal

Bill Lawlor

*T*he long tradition of helpfulness and neighbourliness in Co. Donegal, as exemplified by the cooperative movement, reflects the ethos of the region's Society of St Vincent de Paul, which brings support and friendship to people in need. It is indeed significant that one of the first co-ops was started in Dungloe. It was known locally as 'The Cope.' A relative of the founder, Pat the Cope, was the Donegal people's MEP (Member of the European Parliament).

All of this is highlighted by Terry Gilligan, a member of the Mary Immaculate Conference in Stranorlar, of which he is a former president. He points out that Donegal has no tradition of large estates or big businesses, and in national league terms comes at the bottom in terms of income. He says, 'This I believe gives our members a very special empathy with those we assist and, as we say in our prayer, enables us to "bring our love to the suffering and the deprived."'

Terry feels 'privileged' to live in Donegal and be a volunteer with the Society. He recalls arriving in 'this blessed county' forty years ago and being in the Society there for a similar duration. He remembers that in the initial years his experience was mostly dealing with rural-based people. He says, 'Loneliness was a particular problem, which was relieved by frequent SVP visitation and later by the provision of community centres with adequate transport facilities. The people then had a very obvious faith in the infinite love of their creator.'

Reflecting on the changes in society, he acknowledges that the SVP must also adjust to accommodate these, 'or we will not be as effective as we should.' He continues, 'Younger generations seem not to be as much faith-based as previous ones, and society has become more urban. More and more we have to bring hope – hope and friendship. It is an era of big demands on all of us. It is also an era of opportunity for all of us. Our mission, therefore, is to bring that hope, friendship, love and support to those we serve.'

Love and Disillusion: How the SVP Answered Svetlana's Cry for Help

Bill Lawlor

Sometimes, the dream can become a nightmare. And so it was with immigrant Svetlana, who found herself jobless, pregnant and abandoned by the man she loved.

It was in this situation that the distraught woman, after exploring many other avenues of support, appealed to the Society of St Vincent de Paul for assistance, and her cry for help was willingly answered in a sympathetic and non-judgemental manner that enabled her to overcome her immediate difficulties and get her life together again.

Svetlana arrived in Ireland about four years ago, having previously lived in the UK. Here, she worked as a waitress in the Drogheda area, a happy newcomer, captivated by Irish culture and, of course, the beauty of the Boyne Valley.

But that was not all that captured Svetlana's affections. There was the helpful male friend, who guided her through many workplace difficulties and proved an invaluable mentor. Eventually, that relationship grew into something much deeper and Svetlana fell in love with the Irishman. She recalls, 'We became very close and even dreamed about having a family together. But when our dream started to come true I sadly saw the truth of my situation.'

Indeed, after she became pregnant, reality certainly struck as the love of her life, a man who had two children from a previous relationship, walked away. She had already discovered that because she was working unofficially, without the deduction of PAYE or social insurance from her wages, she was not entitled to receive maternity or any other type of benefit. And, of course, the last strand of her support collapsed with the ending of the relationship with her former lover. Ruefully, she recalls, 'The man of my love loves his family more than he loves me. I was left alone with my fears for the future.'

So, for much of her pregnancy, Svetlana found herself sitting in social welfare and citizen information office queues, desperately seeking relief from her plight. She says, 'None of them could help me. Then I met a local TD who advised me to go to the St Vincent de Paul Society and explain my situation to them. I was full of positive feelings as I walked into the newly decorated office of the Society in Drogheda. At the window I met Valerie Campbell. She really listened carefully to my story. At the end of our conversation she said, "Don't worry. You will be fine."

'Sure enough, shortly afterwards help started to come to my door. The society helped me with food vouchers and with rent money, which was a great assistance. Finally, I could start to think about going into hospital for the birth of my first baby.'

Says Valerie: 'She came to us two weeks before her baby was born. Her rent was due on the following Sunday and she didn't have it, which meant she faced being put out of her home. We contacted the rental agency and negotiated a deal to allow her to remain in the house until her circumstances improved.'

On 2 September 2010, Svetlana's son was born and, to add to her joy, her mother managed to travel from her home country to support the new mum and her first child. Then, with her baby just two weeks old, Svetlana received a phone call inviting her to a job interview. The next day, despite the fact that she was still breastfeeding, she again started work as a waitress. 'At that stage it was a big challenge but I very much enjoyed my job,' she says.

However, Svetlana had always dreamed of going to college to make the most of her considerable talents, and, after a year, her ambitions began to take shape. She applied for and was offered a place on an interior and architecture design course at the Drogheda Institute of Further Education (DIFE). She was enabled to complete the course largely with the aid of her mother and some State benefits.

The 11 May 2012 was a landmark occasion for the immigrant when, at an interior and fashion design exhibition at the local D Hotel, she was able to display some of her artistic pieces for sale. She invited Valerie to the event and, as an expression of gratitude to the SVP for its assistance, she donated a beautiful example of her work to the Society.

'That night was a great success. People were inspired by my work and I was inspired by people,' says a delighted Svetlana, who has now undertaken a number of commissions and is carving out a successful career in her chosen art form. She adds, 'Everyone deserves a chance in life and I was so lucky to get the opportunity that I did. This was not an easy way to happiness, but I know I would not feel so happy now if I had not gone through so much to get here.' She advises, 'Whatever your problem in life, try to find a solution. Never think that things are impossible. Be positive and never stop believing that the world is full of good people.'

The Foreign Nationals who Landed Jobs in Hell

Bill Lawlor

The group of male adults were in a state of fear and exhaustion. Four of them had recent bruising to their faces and necks. Some of them, shivering with cold, were not even adequately clothed.

This was the harrowing scene that greeted a number of Northern Ireland St Vincent de Paul members who answered an urgent request for help on a chilly wet spring morning. The foreign national workers, for whom an anonymous caller had requested assistance, had been dismissed from their legally obtained jobs after continual abuse by their employers. Now, unable to endure any further ill treatment, they had fled their workplace accommodation under cover of darkness and assembled behind church property in search of protection. That was where the SVP volunteers found the distressed men, who said they were concerned that if they stayed and were subjected to further oppression that some of them would retaliate by hitting back to defend themselves, thereby incurring an offence against the law.

Most of the bedraggled, frightened bunch possessed nothing except the largely inadequate clothing they were wearing. While a warm room and some food was immediately organised for them with the aid of the local priest, Conference personnel set about establishing the facts and examining the options for addressing the situation.

In the weeks that followed, however, the migrants and Conference members were to be verbally threatened by representatives of the men's former employer, which presented issues of safety for everyone concerned, including the SVP personnel and their families.

Fortunately, because of a previous case of neglect of a migrant worker and other issues relating to injuries to similar employees, the Conference had established a working group consisting of members, the local curate and a former missionary priest. Contact was also made with migrant families, informal support groups and individuals interested in the welfare of migrant workers. 'These contacts were to play a major part in helping us safeguard and look after the abused workers now in our care,' says a Conference member.

In this respect they ensured the establishment of a vital level of trust between the Conference members and the men in order to prevent further harm being done to them. In addition, the supporters quickly organised overnight bed and breakfast in their homes until the Conference could arrange to accommodate the entire group. Then, as news of the abuse of the workers spread, more help arrived in the form of money, clothes, food and visits from support groups from all over the North. Priests from other parishes also donated money to the Conference and celebrated Masses for the distressed foreigners. Meanwhile, in accordance with the wishes of the latter, the Conference managed to find accommodation that permitted them to stay together, making it easier to deal with them collectively.

In the hectic days that followed, all Conference members met and offered support and comfort to the men, who never complained or argued amongst themselves, despite the fact that they were confined together for days and nights on end. It was also a prayerful time, as it was soon realised that the workers had a strong faith in God and the Catholic Church.

One of the Conference's most active helpers was a former missionary priest who had worked for many years in the migrant workers' home country. He stayed most days and nights with the group and celebrated Mass for them, as well as providing ongoing support and pastoral care. The priest also established contact with the men's families back home, together with government, employment and other support agencies, as a solution to the men's plight was sought.

Then there was a sinister development. Renewed intimidation by the assaulted workers' former employer created huge problems. Two of his senior employees visited the migrants while they were in the care of the Conference. The men, together with SVP members and other supporters, were verbally threatened and told that the building housing the men would also be targeted. The increasing menace meant that the Conference had to move members of the group, sometimes at very short notice, to various other locations. At this stage it became imperative to avoid highlighting the issue because of the necessity for the Conference members to keep a very low profile in order to protect the safety of themselves, their families, supporters and, of course, the by now thoroughly fearful migrants.

An investigation by the PSNI (Police Service of Northern Ireland) of the physical assaults by the employer resulted in a decision to prosecute being left with the injured parties.

A Conference member points out, 'Some other legal issues had to be sorted in relation to us helping the workers, their legal status and also their repatriation. It was deemed that they were dismissed from their employment because the employer made it impossible for them to continue in his employ due to many issues relating to employment law and the assaults.'

Regional union officials and barristers met with the workers to help solve the issues. However, this held out little hope of success as it depended on the workers either taking individual legal action against the employer or returning to their employment.

A condition by the union that the matter be made public so as to maximise the chances of a resolution was not acceptable to Conference members, or indeed the workers themselves, as it was felt that individuals would be targeted for assault. The workers decided to return home, but not to press charges, as this would have meant that they would be obliged to return to appear in court, with little chance of recovering their expenses. The placement agency which secured their employment in the North was responsible, under the agreed contract, for the men's return air fares, but were strongly opposed to honouring the deal. However, after persistent lobbying by the former missionary priest, that organisation eventually agreed to do so.

Of course, for the SVP Conference concerned, the entire affair proved time-consuming and put huge pressure on available funds. Both area and regional councils afforded unhesitating assistance, having been made aware of the seriousness of the situation. The assurances of financial and personal support, as well as words of encouragement from Regional President Cormac Wilson, ensured that they had the confidence to face the difficulties involved.

With the help of the area council, a successful request was made for capital from the sharing fund to which all Conferences in the region contribute. The expenses incurred included the provision of food, shelter, clothing and phone top-up cards (to allow the displaced workers to keep in contact with their families). Finance was also needed to cover the workers' debts incurred since arriving in Northern Ireland, as wages had not been paid to some of them. Families were in debt and the claimants would not be able to get new contracts for months.

The eventual departure of the men evoked emotional scenes of both relief and sadness at the airport, as good friendships between them and their carers had been forged in the weeks spent together. Some of these continue, with the odd text, email or even Christmas card being exchanged. A Conference spokesman relates how they have gained an insight into the culture, language and nature of these people, 'thanks to the missionary priest who taught us so much about dealing with life and people.'

After the repatriation of the workers, efforts were made by the SVP and others to prevent a recurrence of such an atrocity. In this respect, representations regarding the methods of recruitment, work permit types, working conditions and the treatment of sick migrants were made to the relevant authorities. These included local councillors, members of the UK parliament (MPs), foreign consul staff and industry representative bodies.

An SVP spokesman points out that while pay and conditions for foreign workers have improved, they have a long way to go to equal those that apply to UK citizens. He says the Conference members concerned in this case are not seeking publicity for their achievements, but wish to thank all the support groups and individuals who helped to provide care for these young migrants. He emphasises the need to keep some details confidential to protect those involved.

In Harm's Way: Jamie's Story – SVP Helps Youth Flee Paramilitary Threat

Bill Lawlor

J amie was on the run. For weeks he had led a furtive existence, dominated by fear of retribution. As he fretfully boarded the ferry at Larne, the west Belfast youth was aware that he was unlikely to see his native city again for a long time. For the warnings to 'get out of the country or else' were very real. A punishment shooting or even death could be in store for the nineteen-year-old. The paramilitaries behind the threats, taking the law into their own hands, would certainly exact their own form of 'social justice' if he disobeyed.

So how had it come to this for young Jamie?

Plagued by a relentless drug addiction, he had gone on a burglary spree for cash and goods to feed his habit. Although managing to escape legal retribution, his activities had come to the attention of the violent self-appointed 'guardians' of law and order in the North from whom he now needed to flee to safety, probably to the UK.

But how? With family and friends unable to help, and with no connections in Britain, the lad was fearful and desperate.

Then, at last, he got a lucky break. A relative quietly contacted the Society of St Vincent de Paul in the city and explained the plight of the fugitive youth to a member of the organisation. Jamie was subsequently put in touch with an SVP volunteer and moves were soon being made to find him a safe refuge in England, giving him enough money to get set up with a new life there.

The case of Jamie (not his real name) is fairly typical of what St Vincent de Paul has dealt with in a non-judgemental way in Northern Ireland, particularly during the worst years of terror, mayhem and murder. SVP Northern Regional President Cormac Wilson, points out that assistance was afforded right across the religious and political divide to those in difficulty who requested it. He says, 'During the last four decades the civil unrest and sectarian divide has been very well documented in the media universally. It has been claimed that everyone across the religious divide has been in some way affected, and indeed the Troubles have had an immense impact on the Society in the northern region.

'In the North there has always been a perception that the St Vincent de Paul is a Catholic charity for Catholic people. This is obviously a total misconception. In compliance with our ethos we have a Christian obligation, immaterial of who you are or what you are, to offer assistance to anyone and everyone in need. When people have been driven out of their homes and in many cases out of the country by paramilitaries, who can they turn to? The answer has been the Society of St Vincent de Paul. The society in the northern region over many years has quietly and discreetly assisted countless families and individuals to relocate in new homes, very often at a serious risk to our members' own safety and indeed at great financial cost to the Society.'

Cormac emphasises that 'no act of charity is foreign to the Society. This undoubtedly was most prevalent in the northern region during our troubled times. As a result, the Society has earned great respect from our non-Catholic neighbours, which is evidenced by their present generous support of both cash and material donations to the SVP.'

Back Lane Hostel: Working with Homeless People for Almost 100 Years

Bulletin Extract

History

In 1912, the Society of St Vincent de Paul started a temporary night shelter for homeless men at 7 Great Strand Street in the centre of Dublin. In 1915, a new shelter was opened in Back Lane, near Christchurch. Originally this provided low-cost accommodation for working men. As the problem of homelessness grew in Dublin city, the night shelter became dedicated to providing emergency accommodation for homeless men over the age of twenty-six and this has remained its core work ever since.

The accommodation was originally dormitory style. Breakfast and an evening meal were provided, as the men generally left the hostel in the morning and returned in the evening. In 1955, a new oratory was added and Mass is still regularly celebrated there. A major development occurred in 1995 when, with State assistance, a new wing was added and the hostel was reconfigured to give each of the sixty-nine residents a separate bedroom instead of the former dormitory accommodation. Facilities like TV rooms and a snooker room were provided and policy was changed to allow residents to remain in the hostel all day if they so wished. In 2002, an additional six rooms were added by converting old outhouses, bringing the capacity of the hostel to seventy-five.

Latest Development – 2011

The older of the two wings in the hostel, dating back to 1915, although partly modernised in 1995, was badly in need of refurbishment. At the same time, it had become evident that some of the older homeless men and the men with physical or intellectual disabilities the hostel catered for would not be capable of independent living and that, in line with the policy of the Homeless Agency, arrangements should be made to provide long-term supported accommodation for them.

This was another factor driving the need for refurbishment and, in summer 2011, a major reconfiguration of the older wing was undertaken. This provided eighteen ensuite bedrooms and new bathrooms and communal rooms on each floor. The opportunity was taken to modernise the lift, boiler and kitchen and the roof was also upgraded. The total cost of all these improvements came to just over €800,000. Given the economic situation, no State support was available (unlike earlier redevelopments in the hostel) and the SVP had to fund the total cost from its own resources at a time when other demands on it were heavy.

About our Work in the Hostel

The hostel in Back Lane operates twenty-four hours a day, seven days a week, for fifty-two weeks a year. It has an open access policy, which up to recently was for any man over the age of twenty-six, but this age limit has now been lowered to eighteen. The threshold for entry was lowered to cater for homeless men with a range of addictions and social issues.

With the current level of homelessness in Dublin, the hostel is full every night. The aim is to provide a secure and comfortable environment for all residents and to build up a relationship of friendship and trust. Through a system of keyworking on a one-to-one basis, it is hoped to assist residents to deal with the problems which have made them homeless and to help those who have the capacity to do so to break out of the homeless cycle and move into independent living. The current lack of adequate move-on accommodation, coupled with the effects of the economic recession, has ensured that demand for accommodation in the night shelter remains as high as it has ever been. More than 450 men passed through Back Lane in 2011.

How We Operate

The night shelter has always been run through a combination of volunteers and full-time staff. Since 2002, the night shelter has operated through a partnership between the SVP and Depaul Ireland – a sister organisation within the Vincentian family, sharing the same ethos and values as the SVP.

Depaul, which was established by Cardinal Basil Hume, the Daughters of Charity and the SVP in London in 1985, specialises in low-threshold working with homeless people. Depaul Ireland manages six other projects in Dublin and five in Northern Ireland. The twenty-five staff in Back Lane are employed by Depaul and the day-to-day operations are managed by Depaul.

A Conference of the SVP – St Camillus de Lellis – is active in the night shelter, and twenty-five volunteers provide a befriending service to former residents who are endeavouring to settle into independent living. Students from the SVP Conference in UCD assist in the evenings with recreational facilities for the men. Two Daughters of Charity provide pastoral services.

The basic operating costs of the hostel are provided by Dublin City Council and the HSE, while the SVP endeavours, through fundraising and bequests, to fund necessary capital expenditure and to meet other unfunded costs.

The Conference of St Camillus de Lellis in partnership with Depaul Ireland looks forward to being of continuing service to homeless people in Back Lane for as long as these services are required in Dublin.

SVP Helped Dream Come True for Cork Student

Bill Lawlor

A dream comes true for Cork native Denis every day as he goes to work as a top professional in Waterford City.

High achiever Denis (not his real name) is an electrical engineer with a world renowned company, where his exceptional academic qualifications are highly valued.

However, in the words of his parents, all this would have been impossible without the help of the Society of St Vincent de Paul (SVP).

In a letter of thanks to Cork SVP Regional Administrator Padraig McCarthy, they acknowledge that the charity 'has been responsible for the care and education of our son and, as parents, there are no words that can express our humble gratitude.' They say his graduation with honours and distinctions 'would have been a mere dream without the support of the SVP and all the encouragement given.'

The letter goes on: 'We remember our first meeting with the SVP's Mr Ray Cunningham as though it were yesterday and he managed to transform a desperate situation into a proud moment in our lives. Thanks to him and the SVP we have a son who has changed from a boy to a man and will now be able to hold his head up high and achieve goals set as a child.

'As parents we are extremely proud and will always be grateful for your personal contribution to his achievement. In difficult times our hopes were dealt a severe blow and the SVP were there to support and finance a college education for the son of a family they never knew.'

The document also expresses gratitude for the provision to the family of food vouchers and heating oil. It points out that 'work here is not available and, although many applications and CVs have been sent out nationwide and internationally, there has been no success.'

In conclusion, the family says, 'without the help of the SVP we would have been destroyed. Every little thing is accepted by us with great gratitude.'

Cheque in the Post

Bill Lawlor

What a difference a day makes — especially if it brings a much needed cheque in the post.

These were the sentiments of Cork student Josie (not her real name) in a thank you letter to the Society of St Vincent de Paul Regional Administrator Padraig McCarthy.

She says: 'It means so much. The pressure has been lifted ... I get so stressed with anxiety it is sometimes even hard to think straight with worry over having to pay the bills. I can now get books and start to put my best effort into this year so I can progress with my studies.'

She concludes: 'Once I get a job I will remember the kindness of the Society and what it has done for me and my family. I will get a good job at the end of my education. I am sure of this!'

Afterword: Living Out The Eucharist Through Christian Solidarity

John Monaghan, National Vice-President of the Society Of St Vincent de Paul

The Society of St Vincent de Paul, which has been working with the poor and disadvantaged in Ireland for 170 years, was founded in Paris in 1833 by a twenty-year-old university student, Frédéric Ozanam. Along with six friends, he established what they called the first 'Conference of Charity' to work among the poor of the city.

Frédéric and his comrades took St Vincent de Paul as their patron because, as Frédéric said, 'Even the revolutionaries admired St Vincent and forgave him the crime of having loved God.'

Sadly, after a short but eventful life, Frédéric died, aged forty, on 8 September 1853 in Marseilles, France.

Right from the start, the mission of the SVP in Ireland has been based directly on the words and inspiration of Blessed Frédéric Ozanam and St Vincent de Paul.

That mission has three indispensable and intertwined strands:

- To offer friendship and support – both financial and emotional.
- To help people achieve independence with dignity from both the Society and the State.
- To identify the structural causes of poverty and need in Irish society and to advocate for their elimination.

These three strands can be viewed as the legs of a three-legged stool – take any leg away and the stool collapses.

In some respects the first two strands of our mission can be considered as a modern application of the story of the Good Samaritan providing financial and emotional support to those we find lying hurt and bruised on the road of life.

But the third strand goes beyond that because it asks the awkward question of both the State and each one of us: Why is this person lying on the road in this condition in the first place?

Such was the influence and vision of Frédéric that today the Society of St Vincent de Paul has more than one million members working in over 140 countries on every continents.

Significantly, the three core principles of that first Conference of charity – spirituality, faith, community and service – are still the cornerstones of the work and ethos of the SVP throughout the world.

Consequently, being a Vincentian requires the intertwining of these core principles in our daily work. And so each day the members of the Society must try to achieve Frédéric's vision of 'embracing the world in a network of love', and live out his challenge that 'no work of charity is foreign to the Society'.

Significantly, attempting to realise Frédéric's vision and live out his challenge means that the possibilities for Vincentian action are almost limitless. Because being poor is not just about being short of money and material things. It can also mean having a physical or mental disability, being sick or old, lonely or illiterate. And the poor also include those who are made to feel alone and unwanted – for example, immigrants, asylum seekers and migrant workers who sometimes find themselves among others who are indifferent or even hostile. Being poor can also mean being a prisoner, an alcoholic or a drug addict.

And so, Blessed Frédéric knew that service to those in need must promote their human dignity. And that's why he told the early members of the Society that 'Yours must be a work of love, of kindness; you must give your time, your talents, yourself, because each poor person is a unique person of God's fashioning with an inalienable right to respect.'

In effect, he was telling the members of the Society of St Vincent de Paul to look for, and find, the face of God in all those who seek our assistance. But Frédéric was also very strong in his belief that the Society must not only be concerned with relieving immediate need. It must also address the social structures within society that causes that need.

And so he told the SVP volunteers that, 'You must not be content with simply tiding the poor over a poverty crisis; but rather you must study their condition and the injustices which brought about such poverty with the aim of a long-term improvement.'

Frédéric was telling the early SVP volunteers, very clearly, that 'charity and justice must go together', and that Christian solidarity requires active engagement with our neighbours, particularly the poor and the deprived, no matter how difficult or challenging that might prove for each of us.

He said, 'The knowledge of social well-being and reform cannot be learned just from books nor from the public platform, but only by climbing the stairs to the poor man's room, sitting by his bedside, feeling the same cold that pierces him. Because it is only when you have personally experienced these conditions that you can begin to understand and grasp his problems and may then hope to solve them.'

And this is the essence of the work of SVP volunteers today.

Back in the 1830s, Frédéric was, in fact, strongly promoting the concept of Christian social justice, the rights and dignity of every individual and the need for equality of opportunity in education and employment. And all this nearly sixty years before the publication of the first great social encyclical *Rerum Novarum* in 1891.

The Vincentian Ethos and Challenge

In essence, the mission and ethos of the Society of St Vincent de Paul is an attempt to apply Christian solidarity through the application of Christian social teaching in everyday life.

But before looking at how we Vincentians try to achieve this, it's worthwhile reminding ourselves of the origin of the obligation on each of us to show Christian solidarity to one another and particularly to those of our friends, our neighbours and their children who are most in need. It also provides us with an opportunity to remind ourselves of the supports available to help each one of us meet this obligation.

Firstly, it's worth recalling that when Jesus was asked, 'Master what is the greatest commandment?' he replied that there are in fact two – and they are intertwined. The first is to love God with all our heart and the second is to love our neighbour as ourselves.

Consequently, these two great intertwined and inseparable commandments imply that we cannot say we love God if we do not simultaneously love our neighbour in a very tangible way, in other words through showing Christian solidarity, particularly to those most in need. So if we claim that we love God, then we are expected to look beyond our own immediate personal needs, either spiritual or worldly, and actively reach out to our neighbour, whomever and wherever they might be.

Thankfully, Jesus left us with many very clear examples of the personal characteristics required of each of us to help us live out these two great intertwined commandments to love God and love our neighbour, and the Beatitudes are one such powerful source of help and inspiration. (Matthew 5: 3 12)

Relevance of the Beatitudes

Some of the Beatitudes have a particular relevance to the work and ethos of the SVP, both for those seeking assistance and for Vincentians providing solidarity and support:

Blessed are the lowly… not blessed are the mighty and self-important.
Blessed are the gentle… not blessed are the powerful and aggressive.
Blessed are they who hunger and thirst for what is right… not blessed are those who cheat and behave unjustly.
Blessed are they who show mercy… not blessed are those who extract vengeance.
Blessed are those who are persecuted in the cause of right… not blessed are those who are corrupt and prey on people.

Significantly, these Beatitudes are directly applicable in our Vincentian work in the world today. Furthermore, to reinforce this obligation on each of us to show Christian solidarity to our neighbour, it is also worth recalling the response made by Jesus when he was asked by the disciples 'Master what will happen on the last day?' and you will remember that he replied:

> 'Come, you who are blessed by my Father. Inherit the kingdom prepared for you from the foundation of the world. For I was hungry and you gave me food, I was thirsty and you gave me drink, a stranger and you welcomed me, naked and you clothed me, ill and you cared for me, in prison and you visited me.
>
> They replied, 'Master, when did we see you hungry, or sick, or a prisoner, or naked? And Jesus replied 'Amen, I say to you, whatever you did for one of the least of my brothers and sisters, you did for me.' (Matthew 25: 31-46)

The Inspiration of the Gospel Messages

I have always been struck, and greatly inspired, by the fact that throughout the gospels there are many powerful examples of how Jesus, very cleverly, used stories about people from the marginalised groups of his day to emphasise his message of love, hope and above all, solidarity.

For example, consider the role of women in the world 2000 years ago and then contrast that with the prominence Jesus gave to their role in his ministry, often to make a very important point.

For example, the stories of Elizabeth, Martha and Mary, emphasising service; the fact it was women who lined the road to Calvary, highlighting compassion; that it was women who stood longest at the foot of the cross when the men had run away, and it was women who were the first to know of his resurrection, spreading the Good News.

Remember also the many powerful gospel stories highlighting issues of faith, forgiveness and charity. Take, for example, the story of the Roman centurion who came asking Jesus to cure his sick son, illustrating that the power of faith is available to everyone, irrespective of background, even to a soldier of an occupying army.

Or the story of Zacchaeus, the small and hated tax collector. Yet Jesus sought him out from the crowd and spoke to him kindly, emphasising that acceptance, forgiveness and the love of God is for everyone. And then the powerful story of the Good Samaritan, demonstrating so vividly that charity, goodness and kindness is so often to be found among strangers.

Each of these gospel stories, and indeed so very many more, is a clear and striking reminder that as Vincentians we should be very careful of how we treat and judge those we assist, because God can be found in, and will work through, each one of us if we let him.

Faith and Works

As members of the SVP, if our faith is to be meaningful and effective it must be lived out in our everyday life, in the world around us, in Christian solidarity with others, particularly in these difficult times.

The words of St James provide us with another very clear challenge in respect of the attitude and behaviour required of each of us if we are to truly live out Christian solidarity with our neighbour and particularly those most in need, when he said, 'What good is it if someone says they have faith but do not have works? Can that faith save him? If a brother or sister has nothing to wear, has no food for the day, and one of you says to them, "Go in peace, keep warm and eat well," but you do not give them the necessities of the body, what good is it? So also faith of itself, if it does not have works, it is dead.'

So caring for one another, showing Christian solidarity, not just to our immediate family and friends, is not optional for us as Vincentians – it's mandatory. There is a clear pathway for us to meet these obligations and it provides guidance as to the attitude and the actions necessary to help us fulfill our Vincentian obligation to love God and love one another.

Some of the principles of Christian social teaching that relate specifically to poverty and need and the work of the SVP, include:

- *The Recognition of the Dignity of the Human Person* – that a human person is never a means, always an end.
- *Respecting Human Life* – this is about more than not taking innocent human life – it's also about the impact of poverty, exclusion and discrimination on the quality of that life.
- *Under The Principle of Association* – the way we organise society, our economics, politics, law and policy all directly affect human dignity and the capacity of individuals to grow in community.
- *The Principle of Preferential Protection for the Poor and Vulnerable* – this implies that societies must have policies and structures in place that protect the hungry, the sick, the homeless, migrants – those with little power – and even less voice.
- *The Principle of Solidarity* – this means that we are in fact our brother and sisters' keepers, wherever they live and so 'love your neighbour' has a global dimension.

- *The Principle of the Common Good* – this means that we must always be sensitive to the impact that our actions, lifestyle, politics and economics can have on our neighbour, irrespective of where they live in the world.

The Human Face of Christian Social Teaching

While the principles of Christian social teachings are all very noble, they do need a 'human face' to bring them to life. Because, to be effective, they have to be conveyed in words and images that will move the heart of each one of us and inspire us to live out Christian solidarity with one another. In effect, to actively live out the message of love and hope contained in the gospels. Thankfully, we do have many examples of people who did live out Christian solidarity in their daily lives.

People such as St Anthony; St Francis of Assisi; St Francis Xavier; St Vincent de Paul; Blessed Frédéric Ozanam; Sr Rosalie Rendu and many others. They were very much the human face of faith in action, something that each Vincentian is called to be.

Our Challenge

It is my firm belief that it is the duty, responsibility and challenge for each one of us to work for a society, indeed for a world, in which the vision of people like Frédéric Ozanam, the example of so many great saints, and the principles of Christian social teaching are not just considered but actively applied in public affairs.

In essence, we Vincentians must continue to work for a world in which the concept of the common good takes precedence over the specific interests of the powerful, whether they are governments, corporate bodies or individuals.

This will not always be easy. It will at times cost us, both financially and emotionally, because we will encounter powerful interest groups and individuals opposing what we say and do.

But we need to remember the prize if we succeed. That will be the realisation of the message of love and hope contained in the gospels and the immense benefits for mankind that will result from each of us focusing on the common good and trying to live out Frédéric's vision of Christian solidarity in love and justice with one another in our everyday lives.

Surely that's a prize beyond price and well worth working for.